Praise for the plays of Neil LaBute

Some Girl(s)

"No contemporary American playwright is more brilliant than LaBute at dramatizing mankind's passion for ignorance. *Some Girl(s)* is yet another astute demonstration of his uncanny ability to draw pure water from the most poisoned of wells . . . Guy exhibits a deep-seated misogyny that he cannot see in himself but cannot help making visible to others. LaBute is the only one of his playwriting peers to fully understand and dramatize this psychological fillip, which is why his plays are so complex and unnerving." —**JOHN LAHR**, *The New Yorker*

"[A] pungent little morality play." —**JORGE MORALES**, *The Village Voice*

"Some girls get revenge, and some guys deserve what they get. That's the message in Neil LaBute's entertaining, sleekly written new comedy . . . As messages go, this one has been around since *Medea*. But LaBute, who likes to chronicle the underside of urban couplings, gives this version his usual sardonic edge along with some newfound depth . . . Here, he works carefully and successfully to portray a range of sexy, smart women." —**ALEXIS GREENE**, *The Hollywood Reporter*

This Is How It Goes

"LaBute's . . . most sophisticatedly structured and emotionally complex story yet, this taut firecracker of a play about an interracial love triangle may do for liberal racism what David Mamet's *Oleanna* did for sexual harassment."

—JASON ZINOMAN, *Time Out New York*

"This prolific playwright . . . has topped even his own scary self in this unrelentingly perilous, disgracefully likeable 90-minute marvel about race, romance and our inability to know everything about just about anything . . . The only unambiguous thing about this astonishing play is its quality."

—LINDA WINER, *Newsday*

"The most frank, fearless look into race relations from a white dramatist since Rebecca Gilman's *Spinning into Butter*."

—ELYSA GARDNER, *USA Today*

Fat Pig

"The most legitimately provocative and polarizing playwright at work today."

—DAVID AMSDEN, *New York*

"The most emotionally engaging and unsettling of Mr. LaBute's plays since *Bash* . . . A serious step forward for a playwright who has always been most comfortable with judgmental distance."

—BEN BRANTLEY, *The New York Times*

"One of Neil LaBute's subtler efforts . . . Demonstrates a
warmth and compassion for its characters missing in many of
LaBute's previous works [and] balances black humor and social
commentary in a . . . beautifully written, hilarious . . .
dissection of how societal pressures affect relationships [that]
is astute and up-to-the-minute relevant."

—FRANK SCHECK, New York Post

"Will make you squirm in your seat. It's theater without
novocaine [from] an author with a uniquely truthful voice."

—JACQUES LE SOURD, The Journal News (White Plains, N.Y.)

The Mercy Seat

"[A] powerful drama . . . LaBute shows a true master's hand in
gliding us amid the shoals and reefs of a mined relationship."

—DONALD LYONS, New York Post

"Though set in the cold, gray light of morning in a downtown loft
with inescapable views of the vacuum left by the twin towers,
The Mercy Seat really occurs in one of those feverish nights of
the soul in which men and women lock in vicious sexual
combat, as in Strindberg's *Dance of Death* and Edward Albee's
Who's Afraid of Virginia Woolf?"

—BEN BRANTLEY, The New York Times

"An intelligent and thought-provoking drama that casts a less-than-glowing light on man's dark side in the face of disaster . . . The play's energy lies in LaBute's trademark scathing dialogue." —ROBERT DOMINGUEZ, *New York Post*

The Shape of Things

"LaBute is the first dramatist since David Mamet and Sam Shepard—since Edward Albee, actually—to mix sympathy and savagery, pathos and power." —DONALD LYONS, *New York Post*

"LaBute . . . continues to probe the fascinating dark side of individualism . . . [His] great gift is to live in and to chronicle that murky area of not-knowing, which mankind spends much of its waking life denying." —JOHN LAHR, *The New Yorker*

"*Shape* . . . is LaBute's thesis on extreme feminine wiles, as well as a disquisition on how far an artist . . . can go in the name of art . . . Like a chiropractor of the soul, LaBute is looking for realignment, listening for a crack." —JOHN ISTEL, *Elle*

Neil LaBute

In a Dark Dark House

NEIL LABUTE is a critically acclaimed playwright, filmmaker, and fiction writer. His controversial works include the plays *bash: latterday plays*, *The Distance from Here*, *The Mercy Seat* (Faber, 2003), *Fat Pig* (Faber, 2004), *Autobahn* (Faber, 2005), *This Is How It Goes* (Faber, 2005), *Some Girl(s)* (Faber, 2006), and *Wrecks and Other Plays* (Faber, 2007); the films *In the Company of Men* (Faber, 1997), *Your Friends and Neighbors* (Faber, 1998), *Nurse Betty*, *Possession*, and *The Wicker Man*; the play and film adaptation of *The Shape of Things* (Faber, 2001); and the short-story collection *Seconds of Pleasure*.

Other works by Neil LaBute available from Faber

In the Company of Men

Your Friends and Neighbors

The Shape of Things

The Mercy Seat

Autobahn

Fat Pig

This Is How It Goes

Some Girl(s)

Wrecks and Other Plays

In a Dark Dark House

Off-Broadway Edition

A play by

Neil LaBute

Faber and Faber, Inc.

An affiliate of Farrar, Straus and Giroux | NEW YORK

FABER AND FABER, INC.
An affiliate of Farrar, Straus and Giroux
18 West 18th Street, New York 10011

Distributed in Canada by Douglas & McIntyre Ltd.
Printed in the United States of America
First edition published in 2007
First revised edition, 2007

Library of Congress Control Number: 2007937702
ISBN-13: 978-0-86547-983-8
ISBN-10: 0-86547-983-6

Designed by Gretchen Achilles

www.fsgbooks.com

10   9   8   7   6   5   4   3

For Sam Shepard

I have never with these eyes seen anything like you, neither man nor woman.

—Homer

I do not love my Father . . . I wonder sometimes if I do not hate him.

—Robert Louis Stevenson

Some day I will treat you good; some day I will treat you fine.

—Sparklehorse

Contents

Author's Note to the Off-Broadway Edition

It's not often that you get to revisit a new play so quickly;
usually it's a few years later and someone is reviving the thing
or a student digs it out of an old copy of *American Theater* and
you're reminded of what you've done. Not so in this case. As I
mention in the preface to this play, I've spent a great deal of
time wrestling this story to the ground and trying to get it
right. It didn't come easily and now as I look back, it didn't
come very quickly, either. Not for me, at least. This one hurt
a bit.

Knowing that the text was already in the process of being
published, I contacted my tireless editor, Denise Oswald, and
asked if it would be possible to put out a revised edition of the
play when it was reprinted. She was very open to the idea and
since there were significant changes made during the rehearsal
period it seemed both useful and interesting to mark the
occasion by making the two differing versions available.

It's very easy to give out credit when a show is on its feet in
New York and being offered up nightly to critics and audiences;
what wound up there is representative of where the journey
finally took me and, while it is hopefully a seamless whole, it is
actually marked by many stops and visitors who helped guide it
toward its present form. A few worth mentioning: Jason Patric,
who ultimately didn't perform in the piece but had brilliant
thoughts about the story and character; Fred Weller, who tore

up the stage with his portrait of a man scared into a life of acting tough—he was a complete heartbreaker; Ron Livingston, who helped make his shit of a character have that rarest of qualities—humanity; Louisa Krause, for waltzing in and effortlessly creating a sixteen-year-old girl who was both wise and carefree; Carolyn Cantor, for directing the thing under the toughest of circumstances and for creating flowers where there was often only dirt; Jo Bonney, for her usual insight and honesty; all the artistic staff at MCC (Bernie Telsey, Robert Lupone, and Will Cantler), for patting me on the back when I needed it; and especially Stephen Willéms, the amazing, tireless literary manager at MCC, for never letting up. Others who gave much-needed voice and advice to characters along the way include Josh Hamilton, Pablo Schreiber, and Kira Sternbach. More than this, even, but it helps give you a sense of what bullshit it is to put a single name on the title of anything. I'll take the credit because I was there slogging through the mud the whole damn time, but believe me when I say there were a lot of folks down there in the trenches with me.

I hope you enjoy the read. If you have the time, compare and contrast the two—it's been fascinating for me, and I've been in the middle of it. I hope the process will be somewhat enlightening to the general reader, the artist and the scholar; if you can't afford both of these versions contact me at my company, Contemptible Entertainment, in Los Angeles, and I'll try to work something out—a trade or a discount or whatever works. Please don't contact Faber & Faber, as they probably already think I'm crazy—what they don't realize is that they're actually half right. The good news is that most days the

Author's Note

completely sane side of me is in charge and I put pen to paper and keep pushing forward in my quest to make some sense out of all the shit floating around inside my head. Every so often, a nice little play like this one drops out and I'm happy. Hope all of you are, too (hey, it's none of my business but at least I was raised to have manners). On we go, then.

Preface

The Darkness at the Top of My Stairs

This one did not come easy. I've been lucky in the past, writing plays with a frequency that at times would suggest it to be a weekend hobby; it's not, of course, it's hard work, and none of them has ever come without a fight. Obviously, each journey is different—on one occasion a text felt as if it had dropped out of the sky, complete and whole, and I merely had to transcribe it all in one big sitting. Others have been slaved over in pieces, coming in fits and starts as I struggled to make sense of the characters or plot or both. The fact that my work appears with some regularity attests that, no matter how easy or hard the process is, in the end I sit my fat ass down and do the work. You can find as many methods for writing plays as there are teachers and self-help authors out there in the marketplace today, but I've never found anything that worked as well for me as the fine art of putting pen to paper or fingers to keyboard. In 1900, Anton Chekhov wrote out a simple formula for a younger writer, Maxim Gorky, who had approached him asking for some advice. Chekhov's response was pure and straightforward: "Write, write, write!" I've never come upon a maxim that makes more sense than that.

But this one wasn't so simple, for many reasons—starting with the title on down. I had originally decided to call the play "Swallowing Bicycles" after a phrase I'd read in a statement made by Arthur Miller (who was making a reference to critics), and it struck me as a mysterious and singular name for a story. That was during year one of the process that created the text you now have in your hands. The play was originally scheduled to premiere in New York City at MCC Theater almost a year before it finally did; that it didn't wind up happening as initially scheduled was due to two factors—something inside me felt like the script wasn't ready yet and I was also eager for *Some Girl(s)*, a show that had premiered in London almost a year earlier, to finally appear Off-Broadway. This prompted both a shift in programming at the theatre and a change of heart in me. I continued to wrestle with my story, finding the center of it to be more elusive than I had imagined. A new title was born along the way as well, and that's how *In a Dark Dark House* came to be. From the ashes of one script came several more revisions as I continued opening veins to get down to the truth—to the heart of the matter. The title itself was lifted in part from a section of Ingmar Bergman's *Scenes from a Marriage*, which, while originally written for the small screen, is one of the finest dramatic texts I've ever read or witnessed. From all I've read, Bergman appears to have been a lousy father but he's a hell of a writer.

I'm not a very good liar, even though I keep working at it— and this play is much closer to me than some of my others. It's still packed with fiction, much of the story leaping directly out of my active imagination, but there is a kernel of hard fact and truth at the center of the tale. I, too, grew up in a dark house, one that was shrouded in shadows and sadness, and I understand quite deeply what the brothers in the story are going through. I, too, know what it's like to lead a certain part of life in secret, frightened by voices remembered and deeds done. The specifics are of little use to you and best forgotten by me but the core of this particular journey sheds at least a bit of light on my invisible childhood. I lived under the roof of a small house with a man who scared me much of the time, a father whose quicksilver moods moved from euphoric highs to shattering lows. He was probably bipolar and maybe even worse; he had all the charm and chill of an antisocial personality that managed to remain hidden from most people but was on full display in the "safety" of the family home. And though my father passed away last year, he continues to haunt my work and myself—men don't usually fare well under my pen as a result. I like them well enough, I just don't trust them much.

The legacy of my earlier life is that I don't remember a lot about my childhood years. I can look back and see certain foggy images and a handful of lovely moments, but a good deal of that time is lost to me now, hidden behind a veil of menace and murk and quiet. It's not by coincidence that most of my plays begin with the words: "Silence. Darkness."

Another writer whose work is rife with difficult fathers and brothers at each other's throats is Sam Shepard; and it was easy enough to dedicate this work to a man who writes with the skill of an artist and the soul of a survivor. I had the good fortune of reading some of my stories at an event with Mr. Shepard a few years ago—one of those weekends put together by *The New Yorker*—and just to be there, listening to him read aloud from his newest work, was a treat that I'll never forget; to have him react positively to some of my own writing was a dream come true. Hey, you take your fatherly pats on the back where you can get them.

Anyway, did I have a bad childhood? I think so. Was I ever abused? As a matter of fact, yes. Is it all behind me now? On a good day. It's interesting how life evens itself out in the end—I feel like I had a fairly tough go of it early on, but by twentieth-century standards it was probably a cakewalk. I'm still here, after all, so I don't complain much. And you get a play out of the deal, so everything works out in the end. Ain't life funny?

In a
Dark
Dark
House

Production History

In a Dark Dark House had its world premiere May 16, 2007, at the Lucille Lortel Theatre in New York City, in a production by the Manhattan Class Company (MCC) Theater. Director: Carolyn Cantor. Artistic directors: Robert LuPone and Bernard Telsey. Associate artistic director: William Cantler. Scenic designer: Beowulf Borritt. Lighting: Ben Stanton. Sound/Music designer: Rob Kaplowitz. Costume designer: Jenny Mannis. Production manager: B. D. White. Production stage manager: Joel Rosen. Assistant stage manager: Liz Paige.

TERRY	Frederick Weller
DREW	Ron Livingston
JENNIFER	Louisa Krause

Characters

TERRY—a man in his late thirties
DREW—a man in his mid thirties
JENNIFER—a girl in her mid teens

Setting

Three parts—out in the woods

NOTE A slash denotes an attempt at interruption between the present line and the next speaker's line.

First Part

Silence. Darkness.

A manicured stretch of lawn surrounded by trees.
Several areas to sit (benches, chairs, etc.) on two levels,
with stone steps leading down from one to the other. It
feels well hidden from the rest of the world. It is, in
fact.

A man—DREW—staring out at the coming morning. Sound of
wildlife. Maybe just a hint of traffic in the distance.

DREW goes over and checks a high hedge, trying to look
through it. He wanders down a set of steps and studies a
different wall (unseen). Stands on tiptoe.

Another man—TERRY—appears out of the forest. He stands and
watches this for a moment. Silent. Finally:

TERRY Go for it. Make it over and you're outta here.

Startled, DREW turns around and then smiles—he takes one
step forward; TERRY keeps his distance for the moment.

TERRY Or you can fall back on your ass and I'll say I found you
that way. Broken collarbone or however you wanna play it. /
(*Beat.*) Should buy you an extra few weeks . . .
DREW You're funny. / Right! Hey, man, what's up?

TERRY Not much . . .

DREW *smiles at this and waves* TERRY *over—another step from* DREW *but he doesn't commit just yet.* TERRY *doesn't move.*

DREW No, come on, dude, seriously . . . what?

TERRY Nothing. Really. (*Beat.*) And don't say that, call me dude. Grown-ups don't use words like that—not if we can help it, anyway . . .

DREW Whatever.

TERRY That one, either. (*Beat.*) Time to grow up, *dude* . . .

DREW See?! (*Smiles.*) You said it.

TERRY Yeah, but who says I'm a grown-up?

DREW True . . .

TERRY . . . I stopped doing that shit years ago. Growing up sucks.

The two men smile at this. DREW *seems content to grin for a while, but* TERRY *calls it quits pretty quickly. Listening.*

TERRY The road's close . . . the highway or whatever that is. Freeway. / Place is right off the exit, almost . . .

DREW Yeah. / I noticed that—I mean, not today but, you know, like, at some point. Sitting in one of the, ahh, *six hundred* groups a day they make us go to here! / I heard traffic . . .

TERRY Huh. / . . . Probably five hundred yards's all.

DREW Which is really stupid, right? *I'm* not gonna do anything—I was just looking around—but a bunch of the people they've got in here? If they knew *civilization* was just over there—man, it could really get messed up in this joint . . .

Neil LaBute

TERRY S'pose so. Crazies all running up and down the road, dodging cars . . .

DREW Exactly! (*Laughs.*) / That'd be cool.

TERRY Uh-huh. / Pretty funny . . .

DREW Although nobody around here likes it if you use that word, *crazies*. Just so you know.

TERRY Thanks for the tip.

DREW I'm just saying . . .

DREW *shrugs*—TERRY *nods but doesn't say anything.*

TERRY Great. (*Beat.*) . . . So.

DREW Yep. So, so, so. (*Beat.*) So, you gonna stay for lunch or what? I mean, they'll let you in if you want some; chow's pretty decent.

TERRY Sounds good. (*Thinks.*) I need to be back at six, but otherwise, fine.

DREW Too bad, gonna miss movie night . . . It's *On the Waterfront* or some shit. *Black and white.* (*Beat.*) Work?

TERRY Uh-uh. 'S Friday. I'm off Fridays and Tuesdays . . . unless I get hooked up for some overtime, but usually no. / Fridays're mine.

DREW Huh. / Then what, some *lady* . . . ?

TERRY Nah. Got a Little League game at six, I'm doing some umping this year—but I'd be happy to have a bite with you. Sure.

DREW Cool. (*Beat.*) I think it's stuffed peppers or something today . . . plus they've always got their sandwich bar. *Loads* of cold cuts and crap. / It's tasty . . .

TERRY That sounds fine. / Good.

DREW Nice! (*Beat.*) Just like old times.

TERRY Not really. Mom's cooking was the worst. / Christ help us if she did anything like a stuffed pepper!

DREW True! / That's totally true . . . Thank God for Swanson's, right?

They smile at this—apparently Mom wasn't much of a chef.

TERRY Yeah . . . (*Beat.*) So, I'm not sure I can find the right . . . whatever-you-call-it . . . *segue* for.this, so I'm gonna just jump right in—what's going on? / Huh?

DREW Nada. / Nothing.

TERRY Nothing's gonna come of "nothing," Drew, so try again. (*Beat.*) You're in the hospital, little brother, okay? The *psych* hospital, so don't do the whole "it's cool" thing . . .

DREW I'm serious, I'm just . . . you know. (*Tries to grin.*) Anyway, this isn't the real hospital. It's only the *addictions* unit—for us *over*zealous wine drinkers . . .

TERRY I'm not your wife, okay, so I don't need all the bullshit excuses . . .

DREW . . . Terry, I'm not . . .

TERRY I got called to come down here and do some family therapy, Drew, so don't tell me I drove a bunch of hours to have you play games with me. I got a *game* tonight—I need the *truth* from you . . . (*Waits.*) I don't give two shits what you do with these folks up here—that is your business and if the insurance pays for this, then all the better—but do not mess around with me because I'll come over there and kick your fucking ass, I swear to God.

Neil LaBute

A silence grows after this—the dynamic between these two is now pretty obvious.

DREW Great to see you, too, man . . .

TERRY You're a dick.

DREW Yeah. It's my specialty . . . just ask Judy. She keeps a running list of my *failings* in her purse . . .

TERRY She should. / And I don't have time for your dumb-shit act, either, Drew.

DREW *Thanks*, dude. / I know that, bro.

TERRY I really do not.

DREW All right, cool. I get that, and it is totally respected. / *Totally.*

TERRY Then fine. / Drew! God . . . you sound like an episode of one of those, you know . . . some bad TV show.

DREW What do you mean?

TERRY You *know*, those, like, California-type television programs. With the surfer kids and that sort of deal. / 9-0-2-whatever-the-fuck-it-is . . .

DREW No, I don't. / Uh-uh . . .

TERRY Bullshit! "Dude, bro, totally . . ." All your crap. I hate that. (*Beat.*) Did you used to do that in court?

DREW *Sometimes* . . . Forget it, man. Sorry.

TERRY Don't be sorry, just stop. / Stop doing it when I'm around you . . .

DREW Fine. / Okay.

TERRY You're not a kid, all right? You are not some teenager who can run all over doing that, because it sounds stupid. You sound childish, Drew. You just appear goofy and it's a little embarrassing . . . (*Beat.*) You are a grown man.

DREW Thirty's the new twenty . . .

TERRY Yeah, well, you're thirty-five.

DREW So? That only makes me *twenty-*five then. Still young . . .

TERRY Right.

DREW I can't help it—I've got a lot of young people working for me. They rub off on you.

TERRY Yeah, and how does Judy feel about that? Having a husband who sounds like that Tori Spelling girl . . .

DREW We're . . . I try and keep it to a low *roar* around her— this little midlife thing I'm dealing with . . .

TERRY So that's what this is? / *This.*

DREW Hmmm? / What . . . ?

TERRY Why I'm *here.*

DREW No, it's . . . (*Beat.*) What'd they say to you? I mean, do you have any idea why I'm . . . What'd they say?

TERRY Nothing. That you were here and in for a while, that's all. 'S *court*-appointed or something . . . right? It doesn't really matter—you've done so much shit it all just *blends* . . .

DREW I'm sure.

TERRY They said you mentioned some stuff in session that . . . stuff that also would be of interest to me.

DREW Ahhh. Got it.

TERRY Yeah, and so I drove down. I drove here today so that we could . . . you know. Talk about it.

DREW . . . they didn't really say "stuff," did they? No offense, but that's not very professional if they did.

TERRY Drew . . . don't bust my balls, okay? It was something like that . . . "issues" or "problems" or some damn thing. I don't remember now. It sounded urgent so I hopped in my

Neil LaBute

Skylark and dragged my ass down here for *four* hours. / To
be with you . . .

DREW Thanks, man. / I appreciate that.

TERRY Yeah. You know . . . yeah.

DREW Not that I want you to see me in this place, but hey,
that's part of my recovery, to get past the whole *vanity*
thing. Be in touch with the "real" me . . .

TERRY Sounds good.

DREW Don't lie—that sounds gay even to me and I have a far
greater threshold for that stuff than you do . . .

TERRY Well, that's true!

*For the first time in a while the two brothers laugh at
something together.* DREW *suddenly pounces on* TERRY. *Bit of
horseplay erupts—pushing and shoving. Wrestling.*

TERRY . . . Faggot! / Get off me! / Well, you always did know,
right?

DREW Come on! / Ohh, dude! / What's that?

TERRY When something's queer or not . . . you've got this,
like . . . / Yes!!

DREW *Gaydar?* / Oh yeah, I'm the king of that kind of stuff.
The gay-osity of things!

TERRY I figured.

DREW I'm *super*-gay when it comes to all that crap!! / Curtains
and *cologne* and shit . . . I'm a Pottery Barn fag.

TERRY Exactly! / Ha-ha! When you gonna do the ol' "out of the
closet" deal? I still got all that part to look forward to,
don't I?

DREW Fuck yeah! / We'll have ourselves a big party and everything . . . fly Mom out for it, even.

TERRY I knew it! / . . . Sounds great . . .

DREW She can make some *stuffed peppers* for us . . . (*Falls to ground.*) Ahhh!

TERRY . . . and you can help her—being the big queen that you are now. (*Pins* DREW *down.*) / Slip on your Crate and Barrel apron and just go to town!

DREW 'Course! / You got it . . .

The two men slowly stop, letting the moment pass—trying to keep it light. The silence gets uncomfortable.

TERRY Here. (*Helps* DREW *up.*) Anyways.

DREW Yeah. Anyway. (*Beat.*) Nothing like a couple fag jokes to help break the ice, right? / (*Smiles.*) Yep.

TERRY Good times. / So . . . (*Beat.*) What's up?

DREW Nothing.

TERRY Uh-uh, try again. *Now.*

DREW I'm . . . dude, you are a tad *intense*, anybody ever say that to you?

TERRY Don't call me "dude." Really . . .

DREW Whatever.

TERRY I mean it. (*Beat.*) I'm waiting to hear, Drew, so come on . . .

DREW It's not a big deal! I was in for a seventy-two-hour observation and they . . . you know, chose to extend—at *gunpoint.* (*Grins.*) . . . So I'm embracing the thing and I'll be here as long as it takes this time. I *promise.*

TERRY Fine. / That's great, Drew.

Neil LaBute

DREW I'm gonna kick the pills and *every*thing. / Yep. Simple as that.

TERRY Nothing is simple. "Simple's" not even simple anymore . . .

DREW 'S that right?

TERRY Yep.

DREW Sorry, didn't get the *memo* . . .

TERRY Yeah, well, you best keep up, *bro*. World is changing on us, each and every second, so it pays to keep a close eye on things . . .

DREW I hear ya.

TERRY Uh-huh . . . (*Beat.*) So?

DREW *What?*

DREW *stares at him for a minute, a grin rolling off his face in waves.*

DREW You're right, man . . . you are shit at transitions.

TERRY Yep. So I'm gonna ask you again . . . and then after that, that's when I'm gonna get pissed and start in on the angry part of this.

DREW Terry . . .

TERRY *Drew*—why the *fuck* am I here right now? Tell me.

DREW . . . Come on, dude.

TERRY You're pushing it, seriously. You are, like, really pushing me here. Just-say-it.

DREW It's embarrassing.

TERRY I'm sure it is . . . I mean, wait'll this gets around your office! I don't care if it's a *private* wing or not—people are gonna talk.

DREW I don't mind about that. / Who do I know that their opinions are gonna matter to me? Huh?

TERRY Oh, sure . . . / . . . Somebody . . .

DREW *Who?!* (*Grins.*) I don't have a boss, I'm *fucking* rich . . . and my wife and kids've already heard. (*Beat.*) Only person I was nervous about telling was you.

TERRY . . . And here I am.

DREW Exactly.

TERRY And why is that?

DREW What?

TERRY *Why* am I here, Drew? At this place with you, out in the *woods*, right now?

DREW Because, man . . . *Because* . . .

TERRY Good, that's *good*. Get it out.

DREW Don't patronize me, big brother.

TERRY Then just fucking say it, okay? This is getting a little silly . . .

DREW Okay, fine. *Okay.* I need you, all right? That's why . . .

TERRY What's that mean?

DREW I'm . . . what does it *usually* mean? / I'm reaching out here . . .

TERRY I dunno. / Fuck you are.

DREW That hurts, dude . . .

TERRY Yeah, well, then put a bandage on it because it's already starting to stink . . . (*Beat.*) You don't *need* anybody, not one person, and you have proved that a thousand times over, *baby* brother . . .

DREW Wow.

TERRY Uh-huh, wow's right. I get about *two* calls a year from

Neil LaBute

you—and since it's not Christmas or the week *after* my fucking birthday—why don't you go ahead, enlighten me.

DREW Fine. (*Beat.*) I need you to *do* something for me. Is that what you were looking to hear? Huh? 'S that better?

TERRY "Better" is pretty relative—but at least it's honest. You need for me to do you a favor, that sounds more believable than this other . . . shit you've been pitching my way. / Right?

DREW S'pose so. (*Shrugs.*) / Yep.

TERRY So tell me, I'll see what I can do . . . if it gets me back for the first inning, you can probably count on it happening.

DREW *sits down and fiddles with his ID bracelet for a bit.* TERRY *waits, silent.*

DREW I just need you to tell 'em the truth about something, back me up here on some stuff and that's all. / That is it.

TERRY "Truth." / Well, that shouldn't be too hard . . . for me.

DREW What's that mean?

TERRY Well, the "truth" is not exactly your specialty, is it? / If you've got the whatever-you-call-it—*wool*—pulled over their eyes then that wouldn't surprise me. Par for the fucking course.

DREW Dude . . . / You know what, man, forget it.

TERRY Fine.

DREW Seriously.

TERRY Happy to. Take care, pal . . . enjoy the fucking cold cuts.

TERRY *starts off but* DREW *jumps up out of the chair and moves in front of him. Not blocking him exactly, but in the way.* TERRY *steps back.*

DREW Terry, come on.

TERRY Don't suppose you wanna go to your *art therapy* with a broken nose, so I'd step outta my way.

DREW Whatever.

TERRY "Whatever" is what they're gonna use to pick you up off the grass with in a few minutes, you don't back the fuck up and let me pass.

Stalemate as the two men stare at each other—in the end, DREW *steps aside and lets his brother go. Just before* TERRY *disappears,* DREW *speaks:*

DREW It's about Todd. Todd Astin.

TERRY *comes to a quick stop. Freezes. He slowly turns.*

TERRY What'd you say?

DREW I told them about him. 'Bout what he did. / Come on.

TERRY What? / . . . I don't follow.

DREW Todd Astin.

TERRY I *know* his name, you don't have to keep saying the name, okay? (*Beat.*) I wanna know *why* you just said it . . .

DREW It's about when we were kids.

TERRY And?

DREW . . . and nothing, except for all the, you know . . . his . . .

TERRY *What?*

DREW I told 'em about the stuff that we . . . I had to—had to, you know, get it off my chest.

TERRY People don't *have* to do anything. Not at all—live, die,

Neil LaBute

breathe, okay, but other than that, you don't *got* to do much of anything else . . .

DREW Yeah, well, if I wanna keep Judy and the kids in my life, then I do. I *had* to . . .

TERRY Huh.

DREW She made an ultimatum on me, like, a week ago . . . said if I didn't get honest with her about myself—my *history* and all that—then she was gonna leave me. Take the kids and go. Judy does not say shit like that without meaning it. *Un*like me. (*Beat.*) She's at the end with all this . . . surprised she lasted as long as she did.

TERRY Me, too. You got a perfect family there and you piss 'em away . . .

DREW Yeah, well it's over now, dude—this here is the last chance I got, so that's why I need your help on it. I'm coming clean . . . about all my past and everything, that's what I'm saying.

TERRY *nods at this, considering what to say next. Waits.*

DREW What?

TERRY I'm a little lost here, Drew . . . he never did anything with you. Right? 'S what you said.

DREW No, he . . . I mean, yeah. We . . .

TERRY You told me that, *years* ago. / You looked me right in the face and said that he never touched you . . .

DREW I know . . . / I know I did, but . . .

TERRY Then I don't get this . . .

DREW That's what I'm trying to tell you here, Terry . . .

TERRY I warned you about that guy, like, a *billion* times, I told you that you needed to stay away from him and you said you would, you said that to me—said it over and over and *over*. (*Beat*.) Now, was that a lie or not?

DREW It was, yeah.

TERRY I see.

DREW I'm sorry, but yes.

TERRY So, after *all* I did to tell you that, getting sent away and, and—basically tossed out in the fucking *trash* by our dad— you still went off with him? / Hmmm?!

DREW No, I . . . / No . . .

TERRY Bullshit! Bull-fucking-shit!! You said you're gonna get honest, then fucking do it! You and Todd spent time together, right? Even after I specifically *begged* ya not to . . . *Right?!*

DREW NO! Not after, no—before. It was *before* you ever told me.

TERRY What? (*Beat*.) *Drew*, what?

DREW Sorry. It was already too late and so I just, you know, pretended. / I acted like everything was still okay but by that point . . . no, it wasn't.

TERRY Oh. / Ohh . . . shit . . .

DREW I couldn't tell you, I'm sorry. I was too scared about it . . .

TERRY It was *before*?

DREW Yeah, a lot before. (*Beat*.) All that stuff Todd did to me was before that. *Way* before . . .

TERRY You're kidding me . . .

DREW No. I mean, why else would I be in here right now? Talking about it?

Neil LaBute

TERRY Ahhhh, about a thousand reasons . . . Look at your life, little brother.

DREW Dude, I'm trying to get myself on the straight and whatever, okay, so the truth is spilling out—I can see now that a lot of my behavior can be linked to this. Things that happened to me when I was a kid . . .

TERRY Well, that's convenient . . .

DREW Man, what a shitty thing to say!

TERRY I'm not saying anything. I'm not saying it didn't happen—saying it's very *useful* for you to fall back on now . . . so . . .

DREW Hey, look, I don't need you so bad that I gotta sit here and take any ol' crap that rolls out your mouth in my direction . . . (*Beat.*) I'm not the greatest person, fine. I have lots to make up for in my life and with my family, well, all right, I'll work on that, but I don't have to swallow a bunch of your shit, too. I really don't, Terry . . .

This seems to actually land for TERRY*—he nods at* DREW *and lets it soak in. Considering.*

TERRY Look, if that is the truth, that he and you . . . then I'm very sorry and . . . I'll do anything I can to help you here. All I can do. I just wish you would've said something to me, like, back in the day . . . when I could've done something about it. / Saved you.

DREW Well . . . / . . . you can help me now.

TERRY I know, but . . . I just . . .

DREW That's all that matters.

TERRY True. Yeah . . .

DREW It's all the past. I'm just gonna put that behind me and move ahead. / That's what I want . . . I do.

TERRY 'Kay. / 'S very forgiving of you.

DREW You have to, bro. Have to forgive to take the next step . . .

TERRY I see. You learn that here?

DREW Nah . . . people been telling that to me for years! Therapists, a few doctors, but I was, you know, too out there to listen.

TERRY I bet . . .

DREW Keeping it together for the kids, but just barely . . . a little rehab here, some ladies' undies on the floor of the Porsche . . . always just sneaking by. Wanting to get caught, really, but people letting it go, forgiving me, and all the time just handing me a free pass to do it again. A little smoother the next time, so it's harder to get busted . . . and then fucking up *again*. Bigger and better. Hoping that this'll be the one, this time somebody has *got* to stop me! But they don't, they never do. (*Beat.*) Until I ran a traffic light with some chick from work and we're both high—wrapped my *Boxster* around a fucking lamppost—and, well, you know . . . I just watched it come down. My life . . .

TERRY I really don't wanna know all this stuff, Drew. I don't.

DREW It's just *me*, bro. / This is where I'm at now . . .

TERRY Fine, and I'm here to help you . . . / I just don't need all the blow-by-blow, okay? You can save that . . .

DREW Too messy for ya?

TERRY Nah, just not interested.

DREW Well, at least you're honest . . .

TERRY I always have been, Drew. *Al*ways. You probably never noticed because you've been such a lying fuck for most of your life that you couldn't possibly recognize it . . .

DREW Ouch.

TERRY Yeah, not so great being sober, is it?

DREW Not when *you're* around . . .

TERRY Hey, you asked.

DREW Guess so. That's true.

TERRY Anyways . . .

DREW Yep. Anyway . . . you think you can do that for me, talk to those doctors I'm seeing? / Tell 'em about Todd?

TERRY I can, sure. / I'll answer anything they ask me.

DREW Appreciate it. It'll help me out a lot, I think . . . both with them and Judy. She likes you.

TERRY Funny how that works, huh? Married to you and she likes me . . .

DREW Yeah.

TERRY Wonder why that is?

DREW Probably 'cause you don't stay out late and fuck around on her, that sort of thing . . .

TERRY Might be! (*Bitter laugh.*) Yeah.

DREW After a while, wives just seem to be able to tell when you're lying through your teeth . . .

TERRY God bless 'em.

DREW Yep. (*Grins.*) Maybe Judy's just got a crush on you. / That could be it.

The two brothers smile at this one, maybe even a chuckle.

TERRY Right! / Uh-huh. (*Beat.*) So you want me to tell 'em what? These people?

DREW That I'm not making the guy up or anything, that he existed . . .

TERRY Okay. That's easy.

DREW They're telling me that in lots of these cases it's a sibling or some family friend, a parent . . . a figure of some authority. That kinda deal is the usual case. (*Beat.*) Not some dude *drifting* 'cross the country.

TERRY I see . . .

DREW They've even, you know—they asked if it could've been Dad, or, like, maybe . . . you. *Implied* it, anyway.

TERRY Sounds like doctors—heads wedged up their fucking asses . . .

DREW Yeah . . . but I told 'em no. I said it wasn't anybody in our house . . . and it wasn't! / It was *Todd* . . .

TERRY That's okay . . . / . . . Drew, it's . . .

DREW I mean it, though. It was! (*Beat.*) But, you know, can't *prove* it or anything. It's just true, and so, you know. They're finding it . . . "difficult to corroborate." (*Beat.*) Mom came up already but she can't remember *yesterday*, let alone . . . you know.

TERRY Yeah, well, she's been a fucking *ghost* for as long as I can ever remember—how's she doing by the way? / Right . . .

DREW Same . . . back's killing her. The eyes are going. All that shit . . . / (*Beat.*) Anyway, she's no help, and Dad . . . he's . . . whatever . . .

TERRY Dead, I hope. Dead in some fucking alley or hit by a goddamn bus, all I care about that prick . . . (*Beat.*) Anyway, I get it . . . I'll tell 'em anything I can remember about the guy. Dates and names and shit . . .

DREW Good.

TERRY . . . and hopefully that'll help.

DREW It will. / Definitely.

TERRY Fine. / I'm fine with that, then . . .

TERRY *relaxes for a moment now, sits down on one step.*

DREW You okay?

TERRY Yeah, 'course. Just hearing that name again. / It's weird . . .

DREW I know. / Sorry.

TERRY What are *you* sorry about? (*Waits.*) It's just strange, that's all. I haven't thought about him for . . . you know. A while.

DREW . . . Really? Huh.

TERRY What's that mean?

DREW I'm just saying . . . you guys were . . .

TERRY *looks over at his brother, holds his gaze. Finally he turns and looks away.*

TERRY I mean, yeah, he's *crossed* my mind occasionally . . . why wouldn't he? He was one of those people that—you know what he was like—you let 'em in, into your life when you're a kid . . . / You remember what a huge *event* it was when he first came to town . . .

DREW Yep. / Sure. Even *Dad* liked him.

TERRY Yeah! He knew how to do everything and he was always just . . . cool. You know? Could play baseball and swim and helped us out with our chores and all that. (*Beat.*) I'll tell

you what . . . I was only fourteen or something, but I thought
he had a deal going with Mom.

DREW *Really?* / Wow, I never . . .

TERRY Come *on* . . . the way she'd fix snacks for him and
dressing up and stuff? / I noticed all that crap but it was
nothing I could put words to; just spotted the behavior and it
made me . . . I got all angry about it, but not 'cause I
worried about *Dad*—I didn't ever care about that piece a
shit—and he was oblivious, anyway. (*Beat.*) No, see, I just
wanted Todd to be *my* friend . . .

DREW He was. You guys were . . . you spent, like, the *whole*
summer with him! / Practically, anyway.

TERRY Uh-huh. / Except for camp—when the folks made me go
away to a fucking scout *jamboree.*

DREW Yeah, except for that.

TERRY But by then I was, you know—I did a complete one-
eighty on the guy. So . . .

DREW *nods at this while* TERRY *catches himself, not sure how
to proceed. He takes a beat.*

TERRY At that point—the last week or two before I left—he
was being all different toward me. I had this bad feeling . . .
so I tried to tell you, to *warn* you to be careful. And now
you're telling me that he was . . . / You know . . .

DREW Yeah . . . / Yes.

TERRY . . . that it was already too late.

DREW I'm sorry. (*Beat.*) I know he was a big influence on you,
so . . .

TERRY Fuck it. If that's true then he deserves whatever shit gets told about him. (*Beat.*) . . . I can tell these people that much if it's gonna help you.

DREW It would. It'd help a bunch . . .

TERRY And what're they saying about all this? Huh? About you and him?

DREW Well, you know . . .

TERRY No, I don't. I do not. That's why I'm asking . . .

DREW It's what I'm saying . . . I'm *saying* it right now—they blame most all of my behavior in the last year or so on it. / These memories that're coming back up for me—the trauma. That it sorta . . . I dunno, froze me, I guess, kept me in this perpetual age . . . like a *teenager* . . . all acting out and shit, because of it. That what he did to me—all the sexual stuff he tried—had a real effect on my upbringing and is now sort of just pouring out . . .

TERRY Right. / No, I can see that . . . that'd make sense. (*Thinking.*) Sure.

DREW Yeah, and so . . . you know, we're now getting to the bottom of all this and I think it's gonna make a real difference with the judge, on the drunk-driving charges and probably some of the other stuff, too—even the *coke* I was carrying! / Yeah . . .

TERRY That's great, then. / Good.

DREW But that's not why I'm doing it—I really do want to get to the bottom of this. / To put it behind me, what happened. (*Beat.*) I *really* do, man. I wanna get past all this shit that I've been living with. And doing.

TERRY Sure. / No, I mean, yeah . . . I could believe that.

DREW Good. I'm glad.

TERRY And so . . . What do I gotta do?

DREW Just go over some details, fill in a few of the blanks that I left open—you're, like, a couple years older and you can probably remember him a bit better. / Just physically, I'm saying.

TERRY Sure . . . / I can give 'em a pretty fair rundown on the guy, if that's what they're looking for . . .

DREW That'd be a big help, bro. Really.

TERRY Okay. *Bro.*

DREW *moves over and gives his brother a hug. Unexpected—it's definitely a one-sided affair.*

DREW That's so great, dude, honestly! / Very cool of you . . . Thanks.

TERRY No problem. / Least I can do . . .

DREW Awesome.

TERRY Yep. (*Beat.*) So, should we—where are these guys at? Back at the . . . ?

DREW Yeah, the administration building down by the gates there—it's that *Tudory*-looking deal.

TERRY All right. / Fine.

DREW Good. / You wanna eat first?

TERRY Ummmm . . .

DREW We can just grab a sandwich . . .

TERRY I guess. Don't you wanna get this over with?

DREW It's . . . I'm in here now, so it's okay if we wait a little. No rush.

TERRY I've got that game, though . . .

DREW True, but that's not 'til—(*looks at watch*)—like, six, you said.

Neil LaBute

TERRY Right. Okay, great.

DREW Sweet—I wanna show you off a bit! My bro, the working man.

TERRY What's that mean?

DREW Nothing . . . bunch of assholes up in here, you know? I want 'em to get a look at a *real* man . . . a guy who could've been . . . you know . . .

TERRY What? (*Waits.*) Been what? Go ahead.

DREW Nothing. I just mean . . . a dude who listens to his own drummer and that shit. You know what I'm saying . . .

TERRY Huh. (*Beat.*) You got show-and-tell today? That what's going on here?

DREW Come on, Terry, I'm just saying . . . I'm proud of you, isn't that okay? / (*Beat.*) These people are all fucked up for one reason or another . . . it does 'em good to see somebody who is well adjusted. Holding down the same job most of his life, served his country, doing *regular* shit—you'd be, like, an *inspiration* for a lot of guys. Some ladies, too.

TERRY Sure. / . . . Okay, Drew, enough.

DREW Seriously! You have always been a real flagpost for me, even when I was acting like an asshole, didn't call you for months—still admired you. Honest. (*Beat.*) I don't always know how to say that sorta shit . . . feelings that families or, like, a relative'd have but I do get it.

TERRY Thanks. / That's . . . thank you.

DREW Yep. / (*Smiles.*) So, come on, turkey sandwich on me, then we'll go find my shrink and fill him in on Todd Astin . . .

TERRY Okay. Sounds good.

DREW *throws an arm around his brother as they start off.*

DREW . . . Shame we can't find that fucker.

TERRY Yeah, why's that?

DREW . . . Oh, nothing . . .

TERRY What?

DREW Just . . . (*Shrugs.*) Whatever.

TERRY No. *Why?*

DREW Because I'd . . . you know . . . I'd wanna beat the shit outta him, I guess. If I could get my hands on him again . . .

TERRY Little brother, you never punched a guy in your life. Not that I've heard of, anyway . . .

DREW Okay, well . . . that's true. Fine, then I'd have you step in for me. / You do it.

TERRY Ha! / Just like the ol' days . . . I fought every battle you ever had as a kid.

DREW . . . I don't know about that . . .

TERRY Any bully, fucking beatings from the ol' man . . . *all* of it. / I ran interference for you *every* day of our lives, growing up . . .

DREW True. / Second you stopped, my whole life went to pot . . .

TERRY Literally! (*Laughs.*) / Anyways . . .

DREW Exactly! / Anyway, *you* could kick his ass . . . that'd be so sweet!

TERRY Thought you wanted to *let it go* . . .

DREW Yeah, well . . . nothing wrong with a little ass kicking. For old times' sake. (*Beat.*) Fuck 'em up a little, like you did over there in Kuwait to people. / Come on, man—chestful of fucking *medals*?

TERRY *Uh-huh.* / Yeah . . . for being a punk and pissed off.

Neil LaBute

DREW *Any*way . . . it wouldn't bug you so much if it was Todd
Astin, right?

TERRY I dunno . . .

DREW Come on, bro, be honest!

TERRY S'pose not, no. (*Grins.*) Wouldn't hate that myself . . .

DREW Hell yes. I'd murder the dude, you gave me half a
chance . . .

TERRY Yeah?

DREW I mean . . . if I could get away with it, sure. (*Laughs.*)
Then yeah . . .

TERRY Huh.

DREW Drop his ass in a Dumpster and I'd still be able to sleep
like a baby at night . . .

TERRY I doubt that.

DREW 'S true!

TERRY That's a lot of big talk, Drew . . . but I think you'd puss
out in the end. Seriously. / You're more of a "puss-out"
type . . .

DREW Dunno. / You might be surprised . . . I might just do
something that'd bewilder the shit outta you . . .

TERRY Maybe. Figured you might *sue* him—if you were still a
lawyer, that is . . .

DREW You might be *very* surprised what I'd do to that guy,
Terry. (*Beat.*) Took away a part of me, you know? Part that's
not ever coming back, so . . . no, I don't think I'd weep if
that son-of-a-bitch ended up at the bottom of a *lake*
somewhere.

DREW *shakes this off and gives his brother another hug. He
motions toward a distant building, starts off.*

In a Dark Dark House 29

DREW Come on, let's get you fed . . .

TERRY All right.

DREW Maybe we can start a food fight or something . . . /
Have a little fun . . .

TERRY Sure. / Okay. (*Beat.*) Hey, Drew?

DREW Yeah? / It was . . . what do you mean?

TERRY Where did all this happen . . . times he came to you? / I
just wanna . . .

DREW Why?

TERRY I just . . . in case they ask me. I should know some
details. Right? / I mean, if I'm . . .

DREW I guess. / No, that makes sense. Sure. (*Beat.*) . . .
'S the tree house.

TERRY Where?

DREW You know . . . that one tree fort we built, like, down past
the creek? (*Beat.*) He'd meet me up in that . . . In the dark's
where we'd do it—usually when you were off on your paper
route. He'd get me to . . . he'd get all up close to me and
then he'd, he would ask me to take his, make me hold on to
his . . . you know, *thing*, and then I'd have to, I would do all
these—with my mouth I had to, to . . . you know. He would
put his . . . his dick in my . . . (*Cries.*) He would make me
suck on his cock, Terry . . . that's what he did. He *forced* me
to! Forced me as I lay there staring up at the trees. And
he . . . he'd . . . (*Waits.*) 'S that enough? I mean . . .

TERRY 'Course.

DREW I'll go on if you want me to, but it's . . . you know . . .

TERRY No, Drew, that's okay . . . I just . . . / 'S fine.

DREW 'Kay. / (*Wipes his eyes.*) I'm glad.

TERRY Let's get a sandwich and then I'll go, you know . . . tell

Neil LaBute

'em about it. (*Beat.*) I just gotta make a quick call first, that all right?

DREW   Yeah. (*Smiles.*) I'm gonna run ahead and get in line. The best items're usually snapped up pretty fast . . . all the desserts and stuff.

TERRY   Great. / Right behind you . . .

DREW   Cool! / Thanks a lot, bro.

TERRY   You bet.

DREW   I mean it, though. *Honestly.*

TERRY   I know ya do.

DREW   *Thank* you . . .

TERRY   Sure.

DREW *runs off down the path and disappears.* TERRY *stays for a moment, standing perfectly still—he then reaches for a cell phone in one pocket.*

He presses a few numbers but stops. Stands there looking out—as he does, he snaps the cover right off the phone. It's completely broken now.

TERRY *looks down without emotion and plops the pieces in his jacket. Remains where he is. Silent.*

Sound of traffic and the woods.

Second Part

*The grounds have now been converted into a kind of play
area—not for children but families. It's a double green for a
putt-putt course, with two tubes that run from one level to the
next. A hole with a mini-flag down below.*

*A teenager—*JENNIFER—*in shorts and a tank top, ass pointed
out as she works her arm up into one tube. Searching.*

After a moment, TERRY *appears. Dressed casually and with a
putter in one hand.* JENNIFER *notices him watching her—she
gets to her feet. Wipes her hands off on her shorts.*

JENNIFER Go for it.

TERRY What's that?

JENNIFER You can go ahead and play through. / Don't worry
about me . . .

TERRY Nah, that's okay. / No, finish, it's all right. I can . . . I'm
waiting for my car to get done anyway. I'm getting it
"detailed" over there at the . . . Glimmer-King, is it?

JENNIFER Yep. They do a good job . . . (*Beat.*) But I'm just, you
know, doing the *Ajax* thing right now, so . . .

TERRY *nods. Watching her.*

JENNIFER I'm cleaning out the tubes on thirteen and fourteen—
they clog up after it rains.

TERRY Gotcha. (*Beat*.) I think you're talking about Drano, by the way . . . not the other one. Common mistake, really, but only one of 'em'll get rid of your problem. / Blockage.

JENNIFER Yeah? / What do you mean?

TERRY Ajax is just, like, a cleaner. For making sinks sparkle and shit like that . . . Drano's the one people use for clogs. There's other stuff, of course, but Drano's the one you're always hearing about. / On the TV.

JENNIFER Oh. / I see.

TERRY Yep.

JENNIFER What're you, some professional *spokesmodel* or whatever?

TERRY Ha! (*Smiles*.) 'S that what I look like?

JENNIFER Kinda. You sorta have that feel . . . all handsome or something.

TERRY Thanks.

JENNIFER Yeah. (*Beat*.) So, do you do that? Correct people on their cleaning supplies for a living . . .

TERRY Nah, I just know about that one . . . that and, ummm, Liquid-Plumr.

JENNIFER I see.

TERRY I get crap jammed in my pipes all the time out where I live . . . I'm a little off the beaten track, house of mine. / It's on a well and septic.

JENNIFER Hmm. / What's that mean?

TERRY Means *trouble*, most times! I'm not on city utilities, so . . .

JENNIFER Ohh, I get what you're saying . . . Yeah, we aren't, too. At my house.

TERRY *nods without having a response.* JENNIFER *smiles.*

TERRY Sooo—this is your *job* . . .

JENNIFER Yep! Pretty fancy, huh?

TERRY Yeah, nice . . .

JENNIFER I was thinking Harvard and then I got this gig and said, "Hey, fuck that shit."

TERRY Good one . . .

TERRY *watches her as she smiles and takes her bucket over to the high weeds nearby—tosses out the dirty water.*

JENNIFER The world doesn't need any more lawyers . . . it needs a few extra menial laborers. So I'm just doing my part!

TERRY I hear ya. (*Smiles.*) And you're right, by the way . . .

JENNIFER What's that?

TERRY About the lawyers.

JENNIFER Yeah? You spend a lot of time on the wrong side of the law?

TERRY Oh, you know . . . I took Lou Reed's advice and did a little walk out there but nothing too bad . . .

JENNIFER Who's he?

TERRY Nobody. / (*Grins.*) Some singer. Too long ago for you to worry about . . .

JENNIFER Huh. / My dad does shit like that—quotes people and then won't tell me who it is. / That pisses me off.

TERRY Sorry . . . / You heard of the Velvet Underground? (*Waits.*) He's one of the guys in that. And then had a solo thing, too . . . doesn't really matter. I was just trying to be a little funny.

JENNIFER Then you should throw a punch line in there every so often . . .

TERRY Ha! (*Laughs.*) Anyway, point is, I've got a kid brother who's a hotshot lawyer; he's a prick, mostly, so I just lump it all together . . . Excuse my French.

JENNIFER I don't think that's actually French.

TERRY No. (*Beat.*) And *actually*, he's not even a lawyer anymore. Made a bundle when he bought a company out from under a client of his. Apparently that was *unethical* or something, so they asked him if he would kindly fuck off . . . I mean, in so many words. / Disbarred him.

JENNIFER Ahh. / Well, thanks for the info . . .

TERRY Sorry! Shit, forgive me . . . babble on about nothing if I'm around people I don't know . . .

JENNIFER Nah, that's cool. (*Pointing at the pipe.*) 'S either you or dead mice, so . . . you win out by a slim margin.

TERRY Thanks . . . (*Beat.*) You sound a lot like him, actually.

JENNIFER Who, your *brother*?! / Great . . .

TERRY Yeah. / I mean, just a little. He's always doing that, saying all that stuff . . . "cool" and "awesome" and shit.

JENNIFER Well, maybe it was cool. The thing he was talking about . . . ever think of that?

TERRY No. Maybe you're right . . . (*Smiles.*) It's possible; I think he does it to try and *sound* cool, but hey . . .

JENNIFER Doesn't work, huh?

TERRY Ahhhh, no, not really . . .

JENNIFER Got it. (*Beat.*) . . . I know the kinda dude you're talking about. They're in here all the time—usually some *divorced* dad—working overtime to be hip for his kids. / It's pretty pathetic, you're right.

TERRY Yep! / That's *exactly* what I'm saying . . . it's stupid.
I'm always telling him—when I see him, that is—but he just
doesn't listen to me.

JENNIFER That's probably a teen thing, too. Kids never listen.
That's our *job* . . .

TERRY checks JENNIFER *out for a moment, sizing her up—he
takes his time. She's a sharp one, this girl.*

JENNIFER Anyway, you might as well go for it while you wait.
Finish the hole . . .

TERRY No rush. / 'S okay, I'm not really playing. I'm kinda
looking for the owner.

JENNIFER Yeah, but I'm in the way, so . . . / Oh. Well, I'm the
manager.

TERRY Pretty young for a manager. Good for you.

JENNIFER Well, I grew up around it, so . . . it comes natural, I
guess.

TERRY This your place?

JENNIFER Funny . . . (*Beat.*) Sixteen-year-olds don't have
places—we just exist.

TERRY That's true . . .

JENNIFER It's my dad's business. This here. / Yep. / Uh-huh. I
mean, among others . . .

TERRY *Really?* / Your *dad*, huh? / Wow, he sounds like a very
successful . . . something. Entrepreneur type. Guy.

JENNIFER Nah, just means he can't make shit happen, so he
desperately tries a bunch of crap . . .

TERRY Ouch!

JENNIFER Hey, truth hurts.

TERRY Yeah, sometimes it does. (*Beat.*) So it's him I'm looking for, I guess. / Yep.

JENNIFER Okay. / He's not here on the weekends. He works at Big T's Gas-N-Go, 'cause his people're always calling in sick on Saturday, and since I can't sell any beer or whatever. / Not old enough . . . so I run this place for him.

TERRY I see . . . / Huh. And you're the name up on the sign there?

JENNIFER Yup, that's me. (*Holds out a hand.*) Manager of Buddy's Putt-N-Play. My real name's Jennifer, but my dad calls me Buddy sometimes.

TERRY Nice to meet you. It's . . . well, it just is.

JENNIFER Cool. I mean, you too.

TERRY So, your dad must be proud, huh? Of you, I mean . . .

JENNIFER Yep. I'm a chip off the ol' block.

TERRY Well, he's lucky to have such a . . . you know, pretty *chip*.

JENNIFER Aww, shucks, mister . . .

TERRY I'm just saying!

JENNIFER No, thanks, that's sweet of you. *Kind*, or whatever.

TERRY Believe me, I'm not being kind . . . you're a bit of a knockout.

JENNIFER I can yell if I need to . . . I mean, if you're gonna get all *creepy* on me here.

TERRY Well, you better start screaming then . . . (*Smiles.*) Just kidding.

JENNIFER Ha! I *know*. (*Laughs.*) Ya can't fool me—you're a nice guy.

TERRY Pretty much. / Then good.

JENNIFER "Pretty much" is close enough for me. I'll take it. / (*She indicates.*) Well . . . your car's probably done.

TERRY Oh yeah, all right. (*Nods.*) Good . . .

TERRY *stands there, not committing to anything just yet;*
JENNIFER *decides to break the silence.*

JENNIFER . . . Wanna see something?

JENNIFER *walks over to a bottle of soda she's got hidden in the
grass. She bends over and down to the bottle; she puts her
mouth over the opening and stands—turns it up and drinks.*

Tilts her head back down; drops the bottle into her hand.

JENNIFER See? No hands . . .
TERRY . . . Very clever stuff there, young lady. / Yep.
JENNIFER Thank you. / I do gymnastics during school. It's a
    trick I learned . . .
TERRY Not so sure your *dad'd* approve of that trick—showing it
    off to just anybody—but hey . . .
JENNIFER I won't tell if you don't.
TERRY Fair enough.
JENNIFER He's a hypocrite, anyway . . .
TERRY Yeah, why's that?
JENNIFER He does the whole "don't speak to strangers" routine,
    like, each day of the week, but he's always up in the face of
    the kids here. Talking with 'em, I'm saying . . .
TERRY Really?
JENNIFER *Always* . . . everybody who wanders in, he's gotta be
    asking 'em all kinds of shit—it really is nauseating.
TERRY He's probably not seeing it the same way though.

Neil LaBute

JENNIFER What?

TERRY Talking with people . . . he knows who he is, so no worries, but with you it's probably more about your, you know, *safety* or whatnot. He's just doing it because he loves you . . .

JENNIFER Yeah, yeah . . .

TERRY Your mom too, I'm sure.

JENNIFER Well, when you find her, you can ask her for us . . . (*Shrugs.*) It's really just me and my dad now.

TERRY Got it. Sorry.

JENNIFER No big deal.

TERRY Still.

JENNIFER Just the way it is.

TERRY Well, dads love their daughters . . . it's a known fact— anywhere on the planet it's true.

JENNIFER 'Spose so. / Maybe . . .

TERRY I *know* so. / He does, right?

JENNIFER Yes, okay, I'm his little princess and all that crap— it's true! His shining star or whatever . . .

JENNIFER laughs at this and hides her face. *TERRY* smiles and pats her on the back.

TERRY See? / Told ya so.

JENNIFER Fine! / God, it's so . . .

TERRY That's cute.

JENNIFER . . . it's *so* gross, all that gooey junk they say— parents, I mean—when you get older. Just so damn embarrassing . . .

TERRY Hey, it's a hell of a lot better'n being told you're a stupid asshole or something, believe me . . .

JENNIFER Nice. You get that often?

TERRY Just from, like, *birth* on.

JENNIFER Wow.

TERRY Yep. After a while, it sticks . . .

JENNIFER Sorry.

TERRY Ahh, not your fault—unless you're thinking it to yourself right now.

JENNIFER No way. / I think you're pretty okay.

TERRY Good. / Ouch . . .

JENNIFER "Okay" is totally great—geez, you don't know much about teenagers, huh?

TERRY Not really . . .

JENNIFER You got kids? / *None?*

TERRY Uh-uh. / Not that I know of . . .

JENNIFER You want one?

TERRY Only if she's a princess . . .

JENNIFER Ha-ha! (*Grins.*) Seriously, though.

TERRY Ummm, I dunno. We'll see . . . I still got a few good years in me yet.

JENNIFER Maybe . . . (*Laughs.*) Got a girlfriend or anything?

TERRY Nope. Not a one . . .

JENNIFER Ex-wife, then?

TERRY Why "ex"? How do you know I don't have a wife waiting at home?

JENNIFER You wouldn't be yakking away on the thirteenth tee of this shithole if you had somewhere better to be . . . How's that for being Nancy Drew?

TERRY Not too bad! (*Smiles.*) Nah, I'm a single man. And you . . . what do *you* got? Some cute guy, I'll bet . . .

JENNIFER Yeah, I know a few, sure. Boys, I mean . . . that I've

dated or who, you know, wanna try stuff with me—but no,
I'm not hooked up with anybody at the moment. I'm
available, if that's what you're asking . . .

TERRY Thanks, kiddo. (*Smiles.*) What was your name again—
Buddy?

JENNIFER No! I don't know why he named the place that . . .
it's so gay! *Buddy's* just sounds so, so retarded . . .

TERRY I don't mind it . . .

JENNIFER Yeah, well, then you're probably a little bit retarded or
something.

TERRY I like to think of it as *special.*

JENNIFER I bet . . . *very* special.

TERRY That's me . . .

JENNIFER Anyways, I'm Jennifer. I've told you that
already . . .

TERRY Oh, that's right. Jennifer. I do remember that now . . .
sure.

JENNIFER Good. (*Offers up her soda.*) Here . . . Have some.

TERRY No, that's okay . . .

JENNIFER Go ahead, I don't have a disease or anything . . .
promise.

TERRY Ummmm . . .

JENNIFER It's hot out. Go on.

TERRY I can buy one, that's no problem.

JENNIFER The machine is way back there . . . by the clubhouse.

TERRY "Clubhouse." That's a good one.

JENNIFER Whatever! (*Grins.*) You know what I mean . . . the
snack shoppe. Go ahead. Have a swig. / It's 7-Up, so it
won't kill ya.

TERRY All right. / Thanks for the warning.

TERRY *tentatively reaches for the twenty-ounce. Takes a swig.*

JENNIFER Geez, I didn't mean finish it . . .

TERRY Ooops! (*Spits some up.*) Shit . . .

JENNIFER . . . Ooh, that's pretty . . .

TERRY God, I'm *sorry* . . . How suave was that?!

JENNIFER Kinda right up there.

TERRY Damn, that's embarrassing . . .

JENNIFER Don't worry, I do a bunch of shit like that—I'm
practically *famous* for doing goofy crap. / . . . I'm not just
gorgeous; I'm a spaz, too.

TERRY Good to know! / I'm glad . . . and you are, actually. You
really are.

JENNIFER What's that?

TERRY Gorgeous. I mean, for some sixteen-year-old cleaner-
upper person . . .

JENNIFER *Thanks.* (*Laughs.*) You're a riot . . . that must be
another one of your jokes. The "unfunny" kind.

TERRY Hey, I'm just warming up. (*Taking another guzzle.*) Umm,
what is that? Strawberry or . . . ?

JENNIFER Yep. (*Grins.*) Lip gloss. (*Beat.*) I . . . might want
another sip outta there at some point . . . so don't take it
home with you.

TERRY Oh, hey, here . . . have it.

*The two of them stand looking at each other for a moment
without saying anything. Traffic sounds in the distance.*

JENNIFER So . . . what kinda car do you have?

TERRY Nothing special. An old Buick that I fixed up . . .

Neil LaBute

JENNIFER Cool. I like cars.

TERRY That's nice.

JENNIFER Is it?

TERRY Yeah, it's nice to like things . . .

JENNIFER I like all kinds of stuff. (*Beat.*) Fact of the matter is, I'm gonna do that when I get older . . . buy up old stuff and maybe even sell it again.

TERRY Like, what, a junk dealer?

JENNIFER Something like that. You see that show on television where guys go around and judge other people's things? / Tell 'em how much it might be worth?

TERRY Yeah, I think so . . . / Uh-huh.

JENNIFER They call it a "roadshow." That's the name of it on PBS, *Antiques Roadshow.* 'Cause they travel from town to town, I guess . . .

TERRY You're *sixteen* . . . how come you're not watching *The O.C.* or whatever they call it?

JENNIFER I do, I watch all kinds of stuff. Look around, mister . . . / (*Pointing.*) Not, like, *tons* to do in town . . .

TERRY Right. / I get it.

JENNIFER So, yeah, the tube gets a workout at our place . . . and by the way? I'm not, like, a genius or anything . . . but why is it "the" O.C., anyway? It's Orange County, where they come from in California—they say it right there on the show. *Orange County.* I mean, you wouldn't say "the" Orange County, right? Anyways, it's stupid . . . that's not how come I watch the other shows, but still. *"The" O.C.* Dumb. (*Beat.*) 'S probably why it got canceled . . .

TERRY Could be. (*Smiles.*) And so that's your goal in life? To check out other folks' crap and then . . . what?

JENNIFER Just that. Look at it, decide how good it is—tell 'em what they can sell it for or what it's worth . . . (*Grins.*) That'd be pretty neat.

TERRY I guess.

JENNIFER And maybe I can even cheat 'em at it sometimes— you know, like,. tell 'em a false price and then buy it from them. Get an old painting or a chest of drawers dirt cheap . . . without 'em even knowing it—that I practically stole right out from under their noses!

TERRY Nice goal. (*Laughs.*) Jesus . . .

JENNIFER Hey, it's a living. / Kind of like what your brother did . . . right?

TERRY True. / Right! Good memory, kiddo.

JENNIFER Thanks. (*Beat.*) And what do you do, anyway?

TERRY Ummmm . . . I'm sort of a security guard.

JENNIFER Like a *cop*? Eeewww . . .

TERRY Well, not really. I'm unarmed. Can't be a full-on cop because I got a little bit of a *record* . . . Apparently I was a bad boy when I was younger.

JENNIFER Oh. / Hmmm. Interesting . . .

TERRY Yeah . . . / I work nights mostly, and I guard shit for folks. (*Beat.*) From little thieves like *you*.

JENNIFER Ha-ha! (*Laughs.*) You mean, like, at their houses?

TERRY No, not always. Usually I work at a store or warehouse, few construction sites . . . that sort of deal. / Evenings.

JENNIFER Oh. / That's interesting . . .

TERRY Not too much. It's a job, which is okay, and I have days off, which is the good part. I'm not the *deepest* sleeper, so it gives me more time to, you know—do stuff like this. / Drive around. (*Grins.*) *Golf*, of course.

JENNIFER Nice. / Sweet.

TERRY Why is that "sweet"?

JENNIFER Well, otherwise we'd've never met.

TERRY That's true. / I do . . .

JENNIFER See? / Shit always works out for a reason—that's what I think.

TERRY Good philosophy there, lady.

JENNIFER I think it's fate . . . you and I met for a reason.

TERRY That'd be nice if it's the case.

JENNIFER I think it is . . . / Oh, wait, except you're looking for my dad, right?

TERRY Then great. / Yeah. Kinda.

JENNIFER And why's that? Not that I'm all, like, nosy or whatever, but . . .

TERRY Just 'cause. / Wanted to say "hi." Thought I'd drop in, surprise him.

JENNIFER Yeah, but why? / Oh. So, you know each other? I mean, like . . . / Cool.

TERRY Um-hmm. From a while ago . . . / Yep. (*Beat.*) You know what? You've got his eyes . . .

JENNIFER Oh. (*Quietly.*) Huh. That's . . .

TERRY *grins at her;* JENNIFER *blushes and turns away.*

TERRY So . . . how good are you at this?

JENNIFER At putt-putt?

TERRY You could probably kick my ass, right?

JENNIFER Probably.

TERRY Don't be so sure, now . . . I learned it from a pro.

JENNIFER No way.

TERRY True, no, he wasn't a *pro* golfer or anything, but he was good at this. At all sports, really, but this one the most . . . putt-putt. It was years ago, but still . . .

JENNIFER Yeah? / Huh.

TERRY Yep. / We did it all the time when I was a kid. Him and me . . .

JENNIFER So lemme see you, then.

TERRY What do you mean?

JENNIFER Do it. This hole . . .

TERRY *Now?*

JENNIFER Sure. Show me what you got . . .

TERRY You're kidding, right?

JENNIFER Nah, come on! If he was such the superstar, this guy you learned from . . .

TERRY He was pretty damn good.

JENNIFER Okay, then.

TERRY Fine. (*Beat.*) What's the bet?

JENNIFER What bet?

TERRY Hey, we gotta play for *some*thing, if I'm gonna humiliate myself . . . some little treat, the end of the rainbow. / (*Beat.*) You're gonna make it worth my while, aren't ya?

JENNIFER Oh, I get it. / I see . . .

TERRY Yep. (*He smiles.*) So?

JENNIFER Ummm—whatever you say. Up to you.

TERRY Fine—I get a hole-in-one . . . I can have anything I want. How's that?

JENNIFER Like?

TERRY Now . . . come on. Don't make me be all stupid and spell it out. *Any*thing. / As in, whatever-I-choose.

JENNIFER Oh. / *Ohhh*—so that's how it works, is it?

TERRY I knew you weren't ready for this.

JENNIFER Hey, I've *done* plenty, so don't do that "you're just a kid" thing . . . (*Beat.*) I mean, not, like, *every*thing, but lots. (*Grins.*) Some.

TERRY Okay, then there it is. A challenge. I'm throwing down the gauntlet or whatever, like they used to . . . back in olden times. (*Mimes dropping a glove.*) There.

JENNIFER Ha! (*Grins.*) And if you don't? Make it in one, I mean . . . then what?

TERRY I'm screwed.

JENNIFER Sounds like the opposite to me.

JENNIFER *laughs at this—long and loud.* TERRY *joins in.*

TERRY Exactly! That's a good one . . .

JENNIFER See what happens when you add a punch line in there?

TERRY Yeah, it really works, huh?

JENNIFER Sure does. (*Grins.*) So, if you're not able to get it in the hole—let's see . . . all right, here we go. / You miss, then I get a shot at it. I win, I pick. Fewest shots to get it in's the winner . . .

TERRY What? / That's the game?

JENNIFER That is the game. Sound good?

TERRY Not if I was smart it doesn't. Sounds like the cops are waiting off in the bushes there to jump my ass . . .

JENNIFER Ha! (*Laughs.*) That'd be so cool!

TERRY Yeah, *great* . . .

JENNIFER You know what I mean. It'd be so funny if that were true—but it's not. It's just little ol' me.

TERRY My little ol' Buddy . . .

JENNIFER *stops short and looks at* TERRY. *Not happy with that one.*

JENNIFER Eeewww . . . don't say that. "Buddy." / I don't like it . . .

TERRY Sorry, I thought that was your . . . / Isn't that what you said was . . . ?

JENNIFER Yeah, but it's what my dad says to me. He calls me that. That's gross if you do it, too . . .

TERRY Oh, I see.

JENNIFER Right? / It's . . .

TERRY Sure. / No, I understand now . . .

JENNIFER Jennifer is fine. Or J. A few of my friends call me that. J.

TERRY Good, then that's the one for me. Hey, J.

JENNIFER Hey there, mister. Whose name I don't know, by the way . . .

TERRY That's 'cause you never asked. Go ahead, guess . . .

JENNIFER . . . Lance?

TERRY *No!!* Lance sounds like . . . God, like one of those male strippers.

JENNIFER Yeah, exactly . . . must be that smile of yours!

TERRY You sure it wasn't this? (*Does a few moves.*) How 'bout this? Oooh, baby, *ooooh* . . .

JENNIFER *bursts out laughing again—she thinks* TERRY *is the funniest thing around. He may well be, in fact.*

JENNIFER Oh-my-God. That's *so* sick! / Stop! / I'm gonna puke, stop it!! Eeewww!!

Neil LaBute

TERRY What? / I'm amazing, right? / You're loving it, aren't ya? Huh?!

JENNIFER You wish! Don't *ever* do that again or I can't be seen near you . . .

TERRY Then I will stop immediately.

TERRY is true to his word; he stops after one last little ass shake, just for effect—the effect is JENNIFER having another nice chuckle. TERRY smiles, too.

JENNIFER Man, that was *really* ugly. / Awful!

TERRY Thanks. / Thank you, J . . .

A moment between them—TERRY breaks it by pointing back at the steps to the upper level and toward a small mat.

TERRY I tee off from here?

JENNIFER Yep. Unless you wanna go from the kids' spot. / Just to be safe . . .

TERRY No thanks. / I'll roll the dice on this one . . .

JENNIFER Then go for it, Lance.

TERRY does a quick hip shake—JENNIFER laughs again.

JENNIFER STOP!

TERRY 'S your own fault.

TERRY lines up his ball with a hole on the top level. He shoots it through the windmill and he waits. The ball is slow to arrive,

dropping through the left tube and onto the lower green. It
comes to a halt far from the hole.

TERRY Awww, fuck! / Damnit . . .
JENNIFER I'd probably go with *motherfucker* on that one. / Too
   bad for you . . . that's gotta hurt.

TERRY *walks back down and drops the ball into the hole. Stands*
up and grimaces over at JENNIFER.

TERRY Two.

JENNIFER *walks over and puts out her hand for the putter.* TERRY
gives it to her, but keeps ahold of it. He slowly pulls her to him.
A kiss. Simple but sexy—almost perfect and over before either
person can think better of it.

JENNIFER Hey.
TERRY Sorry.
JENNIFER I didn't say it was a problem. All I said was "hey."
TERRY Good "hey" or the bad type?
JENNIFER Which do you think?
TERRY I'm holding out for the first one.
JENNIFER I'll get back to ya on that.
TERRY Hmm. (*Puts hands on her shoulders.*) Maybe
   I should just keep you right here till you
   decide.

After a second, TERRY *kisses the top of her head and then*
*slowly removes his hands—*JENNIFER *takes the putter and*

Neil LaBute

saunters over to the stairs. As she walks slowly up and over to the tee, she trips on the lip of the last step.

JENNIFER See?! *Told* ya . . .

TERRY *smiles and waves her off*—JENNIFER *chuckles, then bends over and drops the ball. She stands and hits it. Without looking.*

They both wait and watch—the ball drops quickly through the first tube and toward the hole. Rolls past and stops.

JENNIFER Shit! / That wasn't supposed to happen.
TERRY *Hell*, yeah! / Ohhhh, baby!!

JENNIFER *glares at him then comes down the stairs to line up a shot. Bends down.* TERRY *makes a "drum roll" sound.*

JENNIFER So funny.

She takes another shot and misses. Throws down the putter in disgust.

JENNIFER Fuck. Awwwww, that's so fucked! / I mean, God!! / Shit . . .
TERRY Oh yeah! / Yes! / Whew-heeww!
JENNIFER Silly.
TERRY Yes, I am. I'm very silly. (*Starts to dance.*) But you still lost . . .
JENNIFER Yeah, yeah, yeah. And you *promised* about the dance . . .

TERRY True. / Sorry . . .

JENNIFER You did! / Whatever. So?

TERRY What?

JENNIFER *So* what's the damage? / Come on . . .

TERRY Oh. *That.* / (*Beat.*) Why don't we . . . you know. Let's get outta here.

JENNIFER Yeah, but to where?

TERRY I dunno. Let's go for a ride.

JENNIFER Just you and me?

TERRY *Us*—let's drive around a bit. Talk about it. (*Smiles.*) Don't worry, we can figure something out . . .

JENNIFER I dunno. (*Beat.*) I'm not s'posed to speak to strangers, remember? / And you could be a bad man . . .

TERRY 'S a little late. / . . . Could be.

JENNIFER *Fine.* Shit . . . (*Shaking her head.*) So, are you gonna go get your car?

TERRY Yeah . . . I'll park in that side lot.

JENNIFER Okay, see you in a few minutes. I gotta go lock up now . . .

JENNIFER *pulls an elaborate key chain out of her pocket—glass ball or something. Twirls her keys and looks at him.*

TERRY That's fancy. What is it? / No?

JENNIFER Nothing. / My dad gave it to me . . .

TERRY Huh. (*Grins.*) And what's your *daddy* gonna say to you taking off early?

JENNIFER Why, you wanna drive by and ask?

TERRY Uh-uh—don't think I do, J. / Nope.

JENNIFER No? / Good. Me either.

Neil LaBute

TERRY Fine . . . I guess it'll be our little thing, then, right?

JENNIFER Yeah. Just yours and mine. (*Gives him a peck on the cheek*.) A secret.

TERRY Yep.

JENNIFER You can keep a secret, can't ya?

TERRY Sure.

She moves off and down a trail back toward the clubhouse.

TERRY *watches her—he swings the putter through the air like a baseball bat. Lets it drop. Stands quietly.*

Sound of traffic and the woods.

Third Part

The space has been converted once more—this time into a bilevel section of manicured lawn. Expensive plants and flowers spilling from various cultivating beds. Several tasteful benches placed carefully about. A statue or two.

TERRY stands by himself, looking out into the surrounding woods. He is dressed in a sports jacket and holds a small plate—it has the remnants of cake and ice cream on it.

After a moment, TERRY looks around and then goes to tuck his garbage inside a bush. DREW—dressed in an expensive suit—enters and watches. He's holding a fluted glass.

DREW Go for it.

TERRY whips around and steps away, a little embarrassed. DREW smiles and holds out his arms—TERRY stays where he is. DREW walks over, gives his brother a half-assed hug.

TERRY Hey there, Drew.

DREW Hi, dude . . . thanks for coming.

TERRY Look, do we have to do this again? I asked you before—
do not call me that. "Dude."

DREW Right, sorry . . . bro.

TERRY Asshole.

DREW I'm just *joshing* you, man! I know, I know . . . I remember
about all the lingo. / Off-limits, I get it.

TERRY Okay, just so you do. / Yeah.

DREW *Totally.*

TERRY You are such a dumbfuck, man. It's really almost hard to
fathom . . .

DREW I just do it to piss you off.

TERRY Yeah, well, it works . . .

DREW Awesome! (*Smiles.*) Hey . . . how's your baseball team?
'S all good?

TERRY I don't have a team, Drew, I'm the *ump.* I told ya. /
Yeah, really . . .

DREW Really? / Oh. I thought . . . huh. (*He shrugs.*) Anyway.

TERRY Yeah, anyways . . . nice to see you, I guess.

DREW You too. / Honestly it is . . .

TERRY Yep. / Good. (*Beat.*) You happy to be outta there?

DREW 'Course! I mean, of course I am . . .

TERRY I bet.

DREW Great to be home and all that, off with my kids and
everything . . . it's fantastic. Absolutely.

TERRY Then I'm happy for ya . . . (*Pointing to the drink.*) I
mean, *cheers.*

DREW Ha-ha! I'm only having the one . . . anyway, it's just some
sparkling cider. (*Smiles.*) *Mostly.* / So . . . (*Beat.*) But
thanks, Terry. It is very much appreciated.

TERRY Oh. / No problem.

*The brothers stand looking at each other—unsure how to
proceed. Listening to the various sounds around them.*

DREW You believe that? I pay a million eight for this house and
a fucking *farmer* next door sells off two of his fields to

somebody else . . . now I've got this *sub*division going on right over there, some shitload of *condos*—fuck! Thanks to that money-grubbing piece of shit.

TERRY That sucks . . . sounds like something *you'd* do.

DREW Yep! (*Laughs.*) Offered the son-of-a-bitch *twice* what he was asking but he held out . . . got it *zoned* and now my land value is screwed on this place. Back in the day I would've sued his ass, but you know what? I'm just gonna breathe deep and let it go . . . / (*Grins.*) 'S the "new" me.

TERRY Pretty cool. / Impressive . . .

DREW Ahh, I couldn't win it or I'd probably still sue the cocksucker.

TERRY Yeah.

DREW I hate that shit! When somebody's actually in the right . . .

TERRY Yeah, that just eats at the heart of you lawyer types.

DREW Hey, hey . . . I'm a businessman now. I'm all *respectable* and whatnot . . .

TERRY Yep. You and Don Corleone there.

DREW Exactly!

DREW *laughs it up at this one*—TERRY *goes over and pulls his plate back out of the bushes.* DREW *waves him off.*

DREW Hey, man, leave it . . . that's what the *Mexicans* are for. Seriously. / (*Beat.*) It's only worth paying 'em if they gotta scramble around and do the dirty work . . . otherwise I'd just use the neighbor kids.

TERRY Nah, it's okay. / I got it.

DREW Dude, they'll probably *eat* it, I'm serious—they'll thank me later.

TERRY No, I shouldn't've done it—it was rude. I know Judy does a bunch of stuff out here, so I'll just carry it back with me. Wasn't thinking. / (*Beat.*) Figure I'm gonna get going.

DREW Whatever. / . . . Already?

TERRY Yeah . . . it's a bit of a drive and I don't wanna get tied up in Sunday traffic.

DREW Everybody's gonna be coming back in this way. You'll be fine.

TERRY Still . . .

DREW I mean, whatever you want, but the kids'd love to see you a bit. They always ask about you . . .

TERRY That's nice. (*Beat.*) Hope they like that stuff I brought 'em. Not much but it's, you know, puzzles—*games* and shit. Children like that kinda thing, right?

DREW Sure. / Of course they do.

TERRY Good. / Great.

DREW But they'd love to *see* ya, bro. That's what I'm saying. Spend the day with you . . .

TERRY Maybe next time . . .

DREW Yeah, but you're here right now . . .

TERRY Drew, *next* time, okay? Just leave it there, would ya? (*Beat.*) You always gotta push things—let it go.

DREW Fine. / I'll tell 'em . . . fine.

TERRY All right then. / Good. See you . . .

TERRY *nods and starts off—*DREW *calls out before he can disappear.*

DREW What's the problem, man?

TERRY What?

DREW I'm just saying, where's the five-alarm blaze all the sudden?

TERRY I told you. I'm tired and I need to get back . . .

DREW You didn't say that before. About being tired . . .

TERRY Yeah, well, I was *implying* it. / My "drive back" and all that.

DREW Right, right . . . / Then go for it.

TERRY Thanks.

DREW *holds out his hand for the plate.* TERRY *slowly walks back to him but doesn't give it up yet.*

DREW I'll take it . . . that way you can go out the side yard. Sneak off if ya need to so badly . . .

TERRY I'm not sneaking off . . .

DREW Bullshit. That's okay, just say it.

TERRY I'll walk right across the fucking *bandstand*, you want me to so bad. (*Beat.*) I need to go—not trying to make a big deal out of it . . .

DREW Fine. I mean, 's just my Welcome *Home* party, that's all, so . . .

TERRY Man . . . *don't*, all right? Do not do that shit or I'm gonna smash you right in the face. You got that?

DREW Whatever.

TERRY That is too fucking true. *Whate*ver. (*Beat.*) You don't care if I'm here or not . . .

DREW Now, where'd you get *that*?

TERRY Ahh, maybe because it was *Judy* who called me, to even

lemme know this was happening—or 'cause I'm standing
around for an hour and a *half* while you're yakking away to
all these other people . . . Maybe something like that.

DREW *Dude . . .*

TERRY STOP IT! Stop fucking doing that! You make me sick
with your silly little act, okay, so shut the fuck up or I'm
gonna put my fist right down your goddamn *throat*, I swear
to Christ!! / I mean, fuck . . .

TERRY *tosses the dirty plate to the ground, angry and
disgusted. He is seething now.*

DREW *cringes and looks over his shoulder, toward the house.*

DREW Terry . . . / It's all right, they can't hear us way out
here . . .

TERRY I don't give a shit who hears us, Drew. I don't know any
of those people . . . *associates* of yours.

DREW The kids, then. I don't want them to get worried . . . /
(*Beat.*) 'Kay?

TERRY God! . . . / (*Frustrated.*) Aaaahhh!!

DREW No big deal. I'm just saying . . . Anyway. Look, if you
need to take off, I understand . . .

TERRY Fine. It's not you entirely—I'm no good at stuff like this.
Meeting folks and all that . . .

DREW You were doing great in there.

DREW *takes another step toward his brother but keeps a bit of
distance too—the guy's not stupid.*

DREW I'm just saying . . . I saw a girl or two trying to come up to you. They were checking you out, bro! (*Beat.*) Seriously, a chick from my office, she came over to me specifically to ask who you were, so . . .

TERRY What're you . . . watching me? Making sure I don't embarrass you now?

DREW Not at all, dude—sorry, man, it's a *habit!*—that was not at *all* the case. (*Smiles.*) I was happy to see you there, talking with Judy and, you know . . . this makes me happy.

TERRY Yeah, well, congrats again on your getting through that program. / *Really* seems to be working.

DREW Yeah. / Absolutely . . . I feel like a *hundred* bucks! / 'Cause two months of being in there . . . that's all I got left.

TERRY Right? / I bet. (*Beat.*) Seemed like a really expensive place.

DREW The best. Best in this area, anyway.

TERRY Well. So long as it works . . .

DREW Uh-huh. (*Beat.*) All that really did help sway the judge, too, so I got you to thank for . . . anyway. Thanks.

TERRY Welcome . . .

DREW I mean it, man—I've done a bunch of stupid shit in my day and, so, you know. Thanks. You saved me . . .

The two brothers stop again for a moment, listening to the sound of construction in the distance. DREW *points to it.*

DREW Listen to that . . . on a fucking Sunday even!

TERRY . . . Yeah, I can hear 'em.

DREW It's the *Sabbath*, for Christ's sake! / (*Beat.*) I mean, for *somebody*.

TERRY Yep. / No rest for the bad guys . . .

Neil LaBute

DREW You mean "the wicked," right? I'm pretty sure it's not just limited to men . . . at least I think so.

TERRY Most women'd disagree . . .

DREW Yeah, well . . . fuck 'em, they can't take a joke.

*TERRY grins at this—*DREW *walks down the steps and takes a look around. Points out a spot overhead to Terry.*

DREW Gonna put a tree fort up there for the kids. Keep saying it, anyway.

TERRY That's good.

TERRY nods at this, thinking for a moment. He looks up at the trees overhead—turns back after a bit.

DREW Yeah, should be. *Lots* of memories, but yeah . . .

TERRY Right. (*Beat.*) Don't do it if it's too hard.

DREW We'll see. Trying to make up for lost time and all that, you know?

TERRY Sure . . .

TERRY now stares at his brother, his mind clicking.

DREW So . . . (*Beat.*) So, so, so. Yep.

TERRY I went and saw him.

DREW Huh? / Who?

TERRY You know. / Todd.

DREW You *what*? You . . . (*Looks around.*) You *saw* Todd Astin?

TERRY I did, yeah.

DREW Where in the hell did you do that? I mean, how'd you even . . . ?

TERRY It wasn't easy. (*Beat.*) Some person doesn't wanna be found, even today it's tricky—all the fucking *email* and computers in the world, if you don't want people to know who you are—you can still do it. Hide.

DREW But you found the guy?

TERRY Oh yeah. (*Smiles.*) 'S the one nice thing about being in security . . . you meet up with a lot of cops and men like that. Investigator types. (*Beat.*) Changed his *name*, but . . .

DREW Wow, that's . . . I don't believe it.

TERRY It's true. Looked that dude right in the eye—fuck, *see*? Now you got me doing it!

DREW Yeah. (*Grins.*) And so, Todd was . . . I mean, what'd he say?

TERRY To me?

DREW Yes, to you! *Fuck* . . .

TERRY Nothing.

DREW Seriously, come on! What?

TERRY Honestly? (*Beat.*) I'm standing there, looking him straight in the face—dead into his eyes—and I'm trying to decide what to say to the guy. 'S over twenty years, right? And he's there in front of me. Takes a glance my way—he lost most of his hair, remember all that, like, *golden* hair of his?—and he says to me, says: "Paper or plastic?"

DREW *What?!* / You dick . . .

TERRY I swear to God. / Seriously . . .

DREW You saw him at, what, the grocery store?!

TERRY Worse. Some fucking Gas-N-Go—that he *owns*. / Yep, runs it, too—he's got himself all set up, not three hundred miles south of here.

DREW No! / Holy shit . . .

TERRY Exactly. / 'S exactly right.

DREW That's . . . / Hard to believe.

TERRY Yeah. Has a little diner, too, and one of those mini-golf courses . . . which his daughter runs.

DREW Shit! He *told* you all this?

TERRY Oh no—stared right at me . . . didn't know me from Adam. (*Beat.*) Like I said: He took my money, he gave me directions, mentioned the weather and a place to eat—that restaurant of his—and that's it. 'S no big deal . . . / (*Beat.*) Only part I hated was that he didn't recognize me, you know? Even after a bunch a years . . . I figured he'd still know when a guy was me or not.

DREW That's . . . I mean, fuck. Really! / I can't believe you did that . . .

TERRY Why? I thought you wanted me to.

DREW Well, yeah, but . . . I mean, I said a *bunch* of stuff to you up there, I still never figured that you'd run into the guy . . .

TERRY I didn't. I went and found him. / I hunted him down . . .

DREW Right, but . . . / . . . still . . .

TERRY Took me, like, *five* weeks but . . . we got him.

DREW We?

TERRY You and me, little brother.

DREW What's that mean?

TERRY I did it for both of us, Drew.

DREW Terry, that's . . .

TERRY Don't worry, I didn't *kill* him or anything . . . if that's what you're all nervous about.

DREW No, I'm not worried, I just . . .

TERRY Bullshit. 'Course you are, but forget about it—it's done now. / I took care of it.

DREW I'm . . . what's that mean? Terry, what're . . . ? / I don't know what you mean by . . . (*Beat.*) Listen, I only wanna know you're all right, that's all—doing that sorta thing can be a real emotional deal. *I* oughtta know . . .

TERRY That's true, you *oughtta* . . . but you don't. You don't because it wasn't you that did it. / It was me.

DREW That's true. / I know . . .

TERRY I'm the one who found the guy. It was *me* in that place, smiling over at him—and he didn't have a *speck* of a notion that I was anybody he ever met.

DREW I'm sorry, bro. I mean, *Terry* . . . I'm really sorry for putting you up to that. It was stupid.

TERRY Nah, it felt good. Like closing a book, really, some book that you'd already read a long time ago, and it needed put back on the shelf—it was a little like that. / (*Beat.*) You should probably do it, too . . .

DREW I'm . . . / Terry, listen . . .

TERRY I'm glad I saw him. I actually am.

DREW Okay.

TERRY Yep. (*Beat.*) Met his daughter, too. She was a really sweet girl . . . *and* you know what he calls her? Guess.

DREW What?

TERRY I said "guess."

DREW I dunno . . .

TERRY Buddy. That's his pet name for her. It's Buddy. / Even put it up on the sign of his golf place . . . Buddy's. Believe that shit?

DREW Wow . . . / That's . . . I mean, didn't he used to call you that. or . . . ?

TERRY Uh-huh. He sure did . . . "Buddy boy."

DREW That's wild.

TERRY Yeah, I thought so. Kinda took me by surprise, that one . . .

DREW I bet.

TERRY *But* a real nice girl, and funny, too! Got that from him, I guess.

DREW Right. He *was* funny, wasn't he?

TERRY Sure was. He was always a comical guy . . . I mean, when he didn't have his *cock* down your throat . . . right?

DREW *nods at this, even tries a chuckle, but it quickly fades away.* TERRY *stares straight at him.*

DREW Yeah. Maybe we should head back over to the tent, bro.

TERRY Nah, I gotta go. I told ya that . . .

DREW Sure, okay.

DREW *starts off again, but* TERRY *isn't going anywhere. He stands there, looking at his brother.* DREW *turns back.*

TERRY Drew—you're not an idiot, so you know, right? I mean . . .

DREW What?

TERRY *Dude* . . . Does that help? If I talk like one of your pals? (*Beat.*) You *know* what I'm saying without me saying it, correct?

DREW I don't, man, no. / Really, bro . . .

TERRY Come *on.* / . . . That's so . . .

DREW I'm not kidding . . .

TERRY Fine. You wanna play these games, then that's fine. It's just . . .

DREW *Seriously*, dude . . .

TERRY Fuck you with that shit, Drew. You and all your *chummy* bullshit . . . we are not friends, little brother, we never have been, so do not act like it now 'cause it makes me wanna barf! I mean it, I hear you say shit like that and, and, and I wanna *puke* my guts up—right up in your fucking face!!

DREW . . . you have got some serious anger issues there, Terry.

TERRY Yeah, you *think*?

DREW I am, like, a hundred percent sure of it. (*Beat.*) Look, if I offended you in some way, then I'm . . .

TERRY Nope. We just don't click as two people, that's all. Shame that we had to end up related, otherwise I could just kick the living fuck outta you and be done with it . . .

DREW Why, man, what'd I do to you? Like *specifically*, I'm saying. Not just 'cause I have money, which I know pisses you off . . . / It does . . .

TERRY Oh, please . . . / *Nooo* . . .

DREW You *know* it does.

TERRY I wouldn't take that shit if your kids crawled up to me and begged me to have it! / *Pleaded* with me to take it from 'em, I wouldn't . . .

DREW Yeah, right . . . / Sure . . .

TERRY I *mean* it. You've got a seriously demented sense of what I consider important, little fella.

DREW Whatever, man. / *Whatever* you say.

TERRY That's right! / (*Beat.*) . . . Trying to *share* something with you and I get this phony "I dunno" shit again— You wanna play that tune then it's okay by me . . . we'll go back

to a call at Christmas and say we're even . . . forget you and
me ever popped outta the same fucking womb's just fine.
(*Beat.*) So long, you little cunt . . .

With that, TERRY *starts off, but* DREW *hops over to him. He gets
in the way, with his arms up.*

DREW Wait, Terry . . . / Come on, hold up!

TERRY *What? / WHAT?*

DREW I'm just . . . Come on, man, I don't wanna part on bad
terms again. We have done that routine too many times,
right? Haven't we? (*Beat.*) Sorry that I didn't call you, it has
been crazy busy since I got back—work and everything—but
I really did want you here, to see you again outside of that,
ummm, you know . . . that place. Not what you'd call my
"finest hour" or whatever . . . right?

TERRY Nope . . .

DREW And if Judy was the one to call you about the get-
together then forgive me, *my* fault, but it was not some
slight to you . . . it's an oversight and I'm standing up here
in front of you saying—honestly—I didn't mean you any harm
by me doing it. (*Grins.*) Scout's honor . . .

TERRY All right then, let's let it go.

DREW Cool. I 'ppreciate it. (*Beat.*) You sure you don't wanna
say goodbye to the kids?

TERRY Nah, I should be . . . (*Beat.*) Drew, I was trying to tell
you something—make this a little easier for you to live with.
Some shit I've never told anybody else. / I mean *no*body.

DREW What? / Bro, then seriously . . . *what?*

TERRY I mean, come on—you did all that schooling, passed the

whatever-you-call-it, *bar* thingie, you are one smart guy, so
please . . . (*Beat*.) Do you really think I just got up one
morning and said to myself, "Hey, this Todd fellow might not
be so great after all"? Huh?! 'S that what you think?!

DREW I, I, I . . .

TERRY I spent the *entire* summer with the guy, Drew. *Every*
waking minute . . . You think he tried anything with you that
didn't happen to me? / I mean, grab me a piece of fucking
stationery off your *walnut*-topped desk there and I'll spell it
out for ya . . . I mean, goddamn . . .

DREW *Terry* . . . / Shit . . .

TERRY Yeah. Now ya got it . . . See, that's not so hard, is it?!
Pretty damn obvious, really, if somebody had taken ten
seconds to give a shit about it . . .

DREW Jesus Christ . . . I'm sorry. / I just . . .

TERRY Why? What for? / I never once disliked it, that's the
funny thing. I didn't . . . You read books they got out there
now, *thousands* of books about this shit—and I've read *all* of
'em—most of 'em talk about how a child is not "*culpable*"—
something like that—why you're not to blame, but you know
what? I loved it, I did, from the very first time that he placed
a finger on me. Yeah . . . it was this joy that I felt with him,
and it's never been like that again with a person, not
anybody ever, which is a little maddening, you know? But
perfect, too. That's why I was always watching him and
Mom and warning you to stay away from the guy. Not 'cause
I was all worried about you or cared so *deeply* for your
safety, 'cause I didn't. All I was trying to do was protect the
one thing that I cared about, which was this guy . . . this
man who came to me and showed me a kindness, this sort

Neil LaBute

of *love*, I guess . . . when I was young. (*Beat.*) "Love," I now see, thanks to you, that he was spreading around like the Pied Piper of . . . wherever the fuck that fella was from. I dunno.

TERRY *stops now, the truth having spilled out of him. He looks at* DREW, *who is frozen in his tracks. Silent.*

TERRY You don't need to say anything.

DREW No, I . . . I'm just a little . . .

TERRY I know I should hate the guy, I do know that . . . but I can't find it in me to, even after all this time . . . Standing there, I'm looking at his stupid fucking middle-aged face and I'm trying to despise him . . . but I can't do it. I just . . . (*Beat.*) I dunno . . .

TERRY *looks off for a moment, trying to find the right words—* DREW *doesn't speak. Just watches his brother.*

TERRY All I *do* know is I'm scared a lot; how 'bout that? Doesn't sound like me, does it? Uh-uh, but I am. Scared of . . . shit, *everything*. Who I am now, what I want or might be capable of . . . all that. So I keep myself to myself, alone, and work hard at not going where I really don't belong. I'm afraid of, like, relationships and stuff, scared maybe I'm a *fag* because of what happened and not hating it . . . all kinds of things . . . (*Beat.*) Know why I'm working the baseball deal this season? Huh? To try and prove to myself that I would never do that to some kid, what happened to me. Really. That is why . . . it's not for my love of the game, believe me! I keep trying to figure out, in little ways, if I'm normal or not, and so far I'll tell you what . . . I just don't know.

DREW Terry . . . 'course you're. You're . . . Fuck, I don't know how to say it, but you're . . . you know . . .

TERRY *nods at this, listening without really believing what his brother is saying.*

TERRY Growing up like we did . . . a father like that one . . . who the fuck has any idea what oughtta be considered "normal"? Right? (*Beat.*) Son of a bitch used to delight in beating me, you know he did . . . the look on his face when he was hitting me . . . fuck him! I don't think he ever got pleasure from Mom the way he did from using his belt on my backside . . . I doubt it. (*Beat.*) So I don't care what I hear from any doctors or, or from some asshole who has a TV show, most afternoons—this guy came to me and made me feel important. Todd gave me something that I had never felt before and cannot find from anything else out there . . . / He made some kinda . . . difference . . . and, you know, hey. So be it.

DREW Terry, I'm . . . / . . . if it matters at all, I'm . . . I get it. I *do*.

DREW *tries to decide how to continue here*—TERRY *keeps an eye on him as his brother searches for the right words.*

TERRY "You get it." 'S that it? Okay . . . (*Beat.*) You wanna know the *real* reason I ran away from camp that summer? Because before I went, Todd made a joke, one about you . . . how he was gonna have to move over to you now that I was leaving. He *promised* me that he was kidding, that he was just being silly, but you know how you are when you're a kid . . . he's practically an adult and the ~~shit~~ crap coming outta his mouth is gospel. (*Beat.*) So, I get out in the middle of this big ol' scout deal, trying to concentrate on *canoeing* and crap like that and I'm, like . . . "~~Fuck~~ Screw this." (*Beat.*) Took me four days to make it home. Had to hitch some, plus the car that I finally took—four *days* so I could warn ya about him . . . but, see, now you know the truth—I was warning you to stay away from him for *my* sake. Because he was *mine . . .*

DREW I'm . . . yeah. I see that now . . .

TERRY *Irony* being, I supposedly came to save you—I mean, in my mind I was also doing that, *absolutely*—but once I was out there, on the run, it was me who needed help. / Needed you to help *me* for once . . .

DREW I tried . . . / I *tried* to . . .

TERRY By telling the old man that I was hiding out in the *garage*? Huh?!

DREW Terry, listen—I was, like *twelve* years old. Just a little kid . . . / I only told 'em that you were, you know, that you'd come home . . .

TERRY Right. / After I asked ya not to . . . *begged* you, in fact! I-*begged*-you.

DREW I had no idea he was gonna react like that! Freak out and, and . . . call the cops and everything. / I don't know!! I was . . .

TERRY How the *fuck* did you think he was gonna act?!! / He used to smack me in the mouth if I dropped a *fork*!

DREW It all happened so fast! We . . . Mom *dragged* me outta there and into the house . . . / Yes, she made me go up to our . . . I, I had to go up to . . .

TERRY No. That's . . . / *No*, Drew.

DREW What?

TERRY Don't.

DREW *What*, Terry?

TERRY Do not do that. Rewrite history.

DREW I'm not.

TERRY Yes, you are . . . because that's the way we do in our ~~fucking~~ [damn] house. We lie about it or we don't say ~~shit~~ [anything]; we clam up and don't utter a ~~fucking~~ *syllable* about things . . . about the real truth. *Yes.*

DREW What're you . . . ?

TERRY I'm-talking-about-you-and-Mom! Okay? *That's* what. The fact that you two could stand there and let me be . . . like I was some . . . ~~asshole~~ [nobody] that you never met before. Even as the cops are asking you . . . *directly* in your ~~fucking~~ [damn] faces, you didn't say ~~shit~~ [anything], either one of you. (*Beat.*) You had the chance to *say* something . . . *anything*—say that not a day of our lives went by without that ~~motherfucker~~ [him] hitting on me or, or that he was . . . that I . . .

DREW . . . Terry . . .

TERRY What? When I finally *needed* you . . .

DREW I did! Terry, that's not true . . . What did you expect?! . . . You know how Dad was when he got going like that! *I* wanted to try and . . .

TERRY Fuck you, Drew, you lying prick! I mean *after.* (*Beat.*) I saw you out there on the lawn as the cops were taking me away . . . you just watched me go. (*Beat.*) You two never said a word. NOT ONE WORD in my defense.

Ever.

DREW No, Terry . . . that's not the . . .

TERRY *That's* the story, Drew—you sold me out to our fucking father and then when you had a chance to do the right thing . . . you hid behind Mom's skirt like a little *bitch* and let 'em drag me off!

DREW . . . No . . . no . . . NO . . .

TERRY You piece a shit—look at you. A glass of *bubbly* in your hand and you're feeling pretty good about yourself, huh?

DREW What does that mean?

TERRY . . . *Means* you're a self-medicating fuck who can sell himself on just about anything! *Always* have been!!

DREW Jesus Christ, Terry . . .

TERRY SHUT UP!!! (*Seething.*) I have been there for you, Drew, tried to help as you've thrown your life away, and you have never even acknowledged that night . . . not *once!*

Silence as TERRY *stops for a moment—*DREW *regroups.*

DREW Look, Dad did all that to you and I'm sorry, I truly am—if you feel like I was to blame. I'm, I really didn't mean for anything like that to happen to . . . How could I? Terry, please . . . I'm not a bad guy, you know that, I'm not . . . at least not when I was *twelve!* (*Tries a laugh.*) Bro, please now—I mean, if we're gonna get all . . . "full disclosure" here—ya jacked a *car*, Terry! Nobody made ya do that, they didn't, and I'm sorry if that was . . . you know. I dunno . . . (*Beat.*) I never wanted him to *hurt* you . . . *God* . . .

TERRY That was nothing, Drew. You know that.

DREW It wasn't *nothing*, Terry, he . . .

TERRY He could smack me all day long and I wouldn't say a thing. I was used to it by then—ohh, and as far as that "car" goes, hell, I could've been outta custody in a few *hours* if somebody would've vouched for me. *Instead* they threw me in juvie for *four* years! (*Beat.*) Never did a thing wrong up until that age—not a stolen candy bar, *nothing*—and I was tossed out of that family like some carton a bad *milk* . . . it was pretty breathtaking, I gotta tell you. To have it happen to you *as* you're watching it and not a *thing* you can do about it to save yourself—not one damn thing.

DREW Yeah, but, you . . . / Okay, fine, I'm just a little confused here . . .

TERRY It's true! / No, I think maybe what you're feeling is guilt . . . which must be an odd fucking *sensation* for you.

DREW What?

TERRY You heard me.

DREW That's . . . for *what*? I didn't do anything!

TERRY Exactly. That's *exactly* right.

DREW Oh, come on!—you wanna talk about the "truth," why don't we at least *mention* the fact that you . . . before the police came you . . . you know . . .

TERRY . . . Go on . . . go on, man . . .

DREW . . . You almost beat him to death! / I'm not saying that he didn't . . . but let's be *honest*, Terry . . . you put Dad in the hospital for *two* months!

TERRY I know. / I know that . . .

DREW Okay, then. So . . ..

TERRY And I'm sorry. I really am. (*Beat.*) I'm sorry I didn't kill him.

DREW . . . Terry . . .

TERRY I will regret that every day for the rest of my life . . . (*Thinking.*) Standing there, in the dark of the garage with him all up in my—the light is spilling in from outside—and after whacking me a few times, he gets right here, real close and sorta . . . he kind of smiles and that hot breath of his . . . he says, "You are outta here, you little fucker," and he looks at me funny, looks and then adds: "Oh, and your boyfriend there's a goner, too." And—for the first time—it hit me. That was *it* . . . this son-of-a-bitch was gonna ship me off and I was never gonna see Todd again. (*Beat.*) So I grabbed him, grabbed him *so* fast that he couldn't even react and I started to . . . I just launched in on him and I . . . I . . . It wasn't even me anymore! He'd dropped to the ground after . . . I dunno, like, a few punches to the head and I got down there on top of him because . . . I mean, I was not through with him yet. I wanted to, to just . . .

DREW . . . . Don't, Terry . . .

TERRY But it was so *good*, Drew!! It was so, so good to see the skin peel back off his face as I was . . . as I hit him there. Goddamn! I'm always gonna remember that. How that made me feel . . . how *great* it felt to almost kill my father.

TERRY *stops now—there's nowhere else to go.* DREW *is off to one side. Silent.*

DREW I'm sorry, Terry . . . I mean, if that is how you've felt for . . . / If that is what you think of me now then I don't know what to . . . say to you . . .

TERRY I'm not angry, I'm really not . . . / Just clearing the air here, little brother, that's all . . .

DREW *starts to say something but catches himself; instead he let's the idea soak in. Overtake him.*

DREW . . . Yeah. Okay, that's . . .

They seem to have reached a detente for now. A separate peace.

TERRY Let's call it a day and I'll head out.

DREW You're always welcome—my casa is your casa or however those people say that shit. / Whatever.

TERRY Dunno. / Maybe ask 'em when they're eating the *cake* outta your bushes.

DREW Ha! (*Laughs.*) You're still a funny guy, you know that? / Even if you walk around with this *dark cloud* thing going on, you're still very comical . . .

TERRY Yeah. / Yep, I am one funny fella.

DREW *drifts over and gives his brother a hug—*TERRY *waits for him to finish.* DREW *smiles and hits* TERRY *on the arm.*

DREW I should pro'ly scoot back, dude. / Yep.

TERRY Right to the end with that shit, huh? / Figures.

TERRY *nods at this and* DREW *reacts silently—shaking his head.* DREW *starts to say something again, stops. Tries again.*

Neil LaBute

DREW Look, Terry, I've been . . . I . . .

TERRY What is it?

DREW It's . . . fuck, bro, nothing, I'm . . .

TERRY Go on. (*Beat.*) Drew, *what*? Please.

DREW I'm just . . . wondered when, you know . . . we might see
you again.

DREW *looks off again toward the house and the party. He
makes an involuntary step, even.* TERRY *watches and waits.*

TERRY Maybe Christmas.

DREW Sounds good . . .

TERRY Get some time with the kids.

DREW That'd be cool . . .

TERRY Kids aren't "cool," Drew. They're all that matters in this
fucking world . . .

DREW I know. (*Beat.*) . . . I'll tell 'em goodbye for you. / I will,
right when I get back.

TERRY You do that. / Fine. Take care.

DREW You too, bro.

TERRY You're an asshole, you're aware of that, right?

DREW I am. You have made it very, very clear for me . . .

TERRY Good. Then we're covered . . .

DREW *nods and starts off—he stops for a moment and watches*
TERRY, *who is looking up into the trees. Searching.*

TERRY Where you gonna put it?

DREW Huh?

TERRY The tree house—which one of these you plan on using?

DREW Oh, I dunno yet. / Haven't got that far with it—just an idea, really.

TERRY Okay. / Sure. (*Points.*) This one's good right up—see that pocket on your maple over there? It's nice.

DREW *goes and looks into the sky where* TERRY *is pointing.*

DREW Yeah, right—I see the spot. / Yep.

TERRY 'S perfect. / Strong.

DREW Uh-huh. I'll keep that in mind.

TERRY *suddenly grabs* DREW *into his arms, pulling him in tightly from behind.* DREW *resists, then slowly gives in.*

TERRY Lemme just hold you a second . . . come on . . . / Stop it, Drew . . .

DREW . . . No . . . / Don't, Terry, you're . . . / Terry, please, I don't wanna . . .

TERRY It's okay, Drew—Drew, stop . . . / Just relax for a second—Drew, STOP-IT! (*Beat.*) I know, okay? I *know* . . . I KNOW WHAT YOU'VE DONE.

With those words, DREW *stops struggling—he almost melts into his brother's arms. Silence as they stand together.*

TERRY I figured it out . . . (*Beat.*) I was listening to you, what you said, and I'm imagining your kids climbing up there and I'm thinking to myself, "Well, they better be a whole lot braver than Drew, 'cause he's a fucking wuss," and then it just . . . (*Beat.*) You and Todd up in our fort . . . that couldn't've ever happened up there—'cause Dad tore it down the summer before. It got all mixed together in my head . . . when you told me, but that's the truth. Isn't it? The old man did that the previous August, when he thought I was having too much fun up there so he tore it down, piece by piece, and made a doghouse out of it. I 'member that now . . . it's all coming back to me. (*Beat.*) Doesn't matter, Drew . . . I promise. It's . . . it's *okay.* I understand why you did all that . . . and I forgive you. I do. 'Cause I know what it's like to be frightened all the time.

DREW *tries to say something but can't come up with words; just keeps sucking in air.* TERRY *finally releases him.*

TERRY *stands there as* DREW *moves to him—burying his head in his brother's shoulder,* DREW *bursts out crying. Long, brutal sobs. Even* TERRY*'s eyes start to well up—he hugs* DREW *with a ferocity that surprises both of them.*

DREW Man, don't remember the last time you ever gave *me* a hug—like, one that you started.

TERRY . . . It's 'cause that might be the first one. Right there.

DREW *nods, still sniffling—he wipes his nose with the back of his suit coat sleeve. Tries to smile.*

DREW I knew that you'd . . . you always see through my lies. / Eventually.

TERRY . . . Yeah. / It's true.

DREW Even my best ones . . . (*Beat.*) Anyway, I'll call ya. I gotta get back up there, but I'll call . . .

TERRY Fine. / Good.

DREW . . . and we can talk about stuff. / I mean, *all* of it. The whole . . .

TERRY Yep. One of these days.

DREW No, I'm *serious* here, Terry—I can say a lot of shit, promise things and all that, but I *mean* this! I'm gonna contact you, okay? I'll call and we can, you know . . . we'll talk. Get all of our stuff out in the open. No matter how hard it is for me, or . . . we'll do that. The two of us.

TERRY Yeah, sometime . . .

DREW Let's try and make it soon, okay?

TERRY All right then.

DREW We can do that, right? Talk? / Yeah. *Soon.*

TERRY Uh-huh. / . . . Sure.

DREW *wipes his eyes and disappears into the woods.*

TERRY *is now alone in the gathering shadows. Finally, he sits. He reaches into his pants pocket and pulls out a set of keys attached to an elaborate key chain—glass ball or something.*

He holds it up and twists it in the dying light. Watches the glinting splinters dance around him as dusk begins to approach.

Sound of traffic and the woods.

Silence. Darkness.

Neil LaBute

Afterword

From Page to Stage

A quick note concerning the short story you're about to read: we've included this bit of prose along with the play because it represents the first time I tackled the themes that are more fully investigated throughout In a Dark Dark House. *The initial version of this story, which I eventually named "Swallowing Bicycles," came about during a flurry of pieces that I wrote for my short-story collection* Seconds of Pleasure. *At the time it didn't seem to fit in with what I was doing with that cycle of stories, so I kept it aside; it also felt as if the characters and plot might be more effectively dealt with in a dramatic way onstage.*

One can observe many changes in the details, both large and small, from the following text to what eventually became the stage play, but it is hopefully still useful and of at least general interest to see the genesis of a talo as it moves from one medium to the next.

If nothing else, you can delight in the knowledge that I spent quite a few hours sitting in a parking lot so that you could have something fun and surprising to read.

Swallowing Bicycles

"I'm going to kill him." That's what keeps running through my head as I'm sitting there in my rental car, parked at one shadow-filled end of an Albertson's parking lot. To be honest, I've thought of nothing else for the past few weeks, and today is the day. A man is about to die because of me.

It's barely ten minutes of two right now—I don't know how I've arrived so early but it must be nerves. I know he doesn't get off his shift (he works mornings) until three-thirty but that's all right; I can wait. It's warm enough to turn the car off, let it heat up in the sun that broke through the clouds only an hour ago. I'd probably have to shut down the engine anyway, even if it was freezing, since a running automobile will always attract the attention of somebody after a while. A box boy—do they still even call them that?—or a housewife running in to pick up a gallon of milk might remember the maroon Focus sitting under one of those little trees that they plant in the cement islands to spruce up the place, and the police would have their first clue. The first crumb on their trail of evidence that would ultimately lead them back to me. So I turn the ignition to "off" and sit back to wait.

It's been nearly six months since I first went to the hospital, six months since I sat with my brother and heard his tear-filled explanation of why he's found himself back in a place like that. Court-appointed to a rehab unit at a beautiful old hospital set off from the road by half a football field of real estate out front and shielded from curious eyes by a stretch of thick pines. The reason, he tells me, for this particular visit has been erratic behavior at work—manic calls overheard by assistants, soaring costs on his personal expense account, etc.—that has finally surpassed his worth as an employee. Thankfully, he works with an old friend of the family (classmate of mine, actually, who went off and made good in the world of business) and his company has an outstanding health program that includes benefits in the areas of mental illness, addictions, and the like. My brother has already racked up weeks and weeks of "sick" time spent in homes trying to fend his dependence on prescription painkillers and alcohol but this return visit has some serious implications to it. His work, family, everything hinges on his being able to fend off these demons and return to the slow death of responsible adulthood. That, and the fact that he wrapped his Boxster around a tree in his neighborhood as he was going about ninety (injuring himself and killing a wandering cocker spaniel). Two days later he packed up and checked in to Whispering Pines for an extended stay, and that's how I got pulled into the picture.

About then the dreams began.

At the hospital and under the constant barrage of therapy—along with a threat from his wife, Janie, that she was leaving and taking the kids back to Michigan—a series of sharp memories about a person from our youth began to come back to my kid brother. This boy who spent one summer with us, working for our dad on the farm that we were born on. He was probably six years older than us, maybe a little more, but he had the youthful vigor of a teenager and was a great friend to me at that time. Growing up in a household where you are the brunt of your father's frustration and anger is no easy thing— I've still got marks on my back from where the man beat me with anything he could get his hands on—and this guy (Todd was his name) was both a friend and mentor to me. Taught me how to golf and (secretly) how to at least steer a car, and even let me have my first sip of beer. A long, slow pull on a bottle of Budweiser that he kept in his room. And now my brother is saying publicly that this person made advances to him, took advantage of him in a sexual way all during that time, and it is these memories that are haunting him and his work—ruining his life. And I believe him. Something in his eyes tells me that this is the truth, and I visit him at the hospital and tell his doctors all that I remember about Todd, this stranger from my youth whom I longed to be like and respected greatly as a person—I tell them detail upon detail about that fragile summer from our boyhood.

The result is my little brother escapes the dull, sightless arm of the law and gets off with a bit of community service, and he looks at me now at various gatherings with the goofy admiration of the family dog. He and I have never really been close—I haven't wanted much to do with anybody connected with those early years of my life—and I'd rather swallow a bicycle or put a bazooka to my temple than speak to my father (who is living over in Arizona somewhere after my mom finally divorced him, decades after it would've done any of us a speck of good), but it felt nice to help someone out for once. I've spent most of my adult life hiding from people, hiding in plain sight by being quiet and doing my work and never raising my hand. For the most part I live in a ghost world where I pay taxes and work the night shift and drift through shopping malls and movie theaters with my head down and what appears to be a vague sense of purpose. I was a good kid when I was young, most folks would attest to that, but the old man beat most of that goodness out of me and now I'm just okay, and okay is pretty dangerous when it gets pushed even slightly in the wrong direction.

And that's why I'm sitting here in a rented Ford Focus waiting for Todd—grown up and a father of two, from what I can gather—to walk out of Albertson's and head to his own automobile. I'm going to kill him today, follow him home and stab him to death in his own driveway (his daughters are at gymnastics with their mother on Thursdays), and be gone and out of state again before anybody knows better. It took me several weeks to track him down and another three days of lazy questions around town to figure out his various routines but now I'm ready. I'm prepared for murder.

I check my watch and I see the hands are perched around three-fifteen. I wonder what it would feel like to know that you have so little time left in your life, only moments now before you die, and that's when I see him again. Walking slowly toward his older-model Honda out in the employee parking area. Carrying two bags of groceries and trying to talk on his cell phone. His hair is thinner now, worn a bit longer to disguise its demise, but still as blond (almost golden) as it was when we first met. He's put on a little weight as well but he moves with a certain grace—it could be my imagination—that I can easily recall from that summer. I drift for a moment, knowing that the blade I drive into this man will seal my own secret life with him safely away and that I, too, may eventually find peace because of it. I try hard to remind myself that I'm doing this for my brother but I can't really make that one stick; it is only jealousy I feel toward my sibling and what has happened to him as a child. Not pity. No, this killing will be as much for me as for anyone else, a death caused by what turns out to be a jilted lover. Me. It is a crime of passion—desire for a man who stole my heart when I was fourteen years old and never gave it back—disguised as a random knifing and robbery. Shocking, the things we find ourselves capable of.

The Civic rumbles forward and begins to pull out, signaling a left. I sit forward and turn the key as the engine quickly catches. Roaring to life. I'm offered a glimpse of myself in the mirror but I turn it sharply away with a free hand. Anonymous now as I drift slowly along behind this man I've always loved but never until now been able to face again.

The two cars slip out of the parking lot and away into traffic, disappearing from view a moment or two later.